EXPLORE MISSISSIPPI GUIDE

OWEN BORVILLE

TABLE OF CONTENTS

THE HISTORIC TRIANGLE OF SOUTHWEST MISSISSIPPI

SOUTHEAST MISSISSIPPI REGION

THE COASTAL MISSISSIPPI REGION

THE DELTA REGION OF NORTHWEST MISSISSIPPI

THE HILLS OF NORTH MISSISSIPPI

THE PINES OF EAST MISSISSIPPI

ABOUT THE AUTHOR

Having lived in other states including California, Arkansas, and South Carolina, I choose to call Mississippi home and have lived here since age 12. I have also travelled across the United States including the Southeast, the Northwest and the Southwest. I chose to write this book not only to learn more about Mississippi but also to tell others about this great state. I also love telling native Mississippians things about their state that they did not know and telling them about places that they did not know about. So it was a pleasure to take on this project. I hope readers enjoy this book as much as I enjoyed producing it.

INTRODUCTION

This book is intended as a travel guide for native Mississippians, for natives of other states, and even natives other countries. Mississippi natives will enjoy reading about their home state and about the many places to see and things to do. Non-natives will be introduced to the state and will be surprised to learn about the attractions in Mississippi.

Mississippi is a diverse state. From the towns along the Mississippi River floodplain that are among the oldest in the state to the urban center of Jackson to the rolling hills of North Mississippi, one can find different physical landforms and a variety of cultural attractions. The Pines region of East Mississippi and the Coastal region offer even more diverse landscapes and a variety of attractions.

So what is great about Mississippi? With such a diverse collection of attractions, visitors can find plenty of things to do. But even more notable than the diversity of attractions is the friendliness of the people. Mississippi is known for its hospitality. So coming to Mississippi is like coming home.

In addition to the diversity of attractions, one will recognize the uniqueness of the attractions. Places like the Delta region and its Blues culture are not found anywhere else. Not only are Mississippians known for their friendliness, but they take pride in their state. So before making a judgment about Mississippi, take the time to get to know the people, the history, the culture, and the traditions of this great state. One is sure to find something interesting and enjoyable to do here in Mississippi.

When it comes to tourism, Mississippi offers something for everyone. From art museums and performing arts centers to science museums, zoos and aquariums, botanical gardens and arboretums, Mississippi offers most of the attractions that other states offer. In addition to man-made attractions, Mississippi has many natural attractions including the coast, rivers, lakes, parks, and diverse wildlife. Only 23 of 50 states have a coastline facing an ocean, so Mississippi is fortunate to be one of those. Mississippi's coastline features the world's largest man-made beach.

Mississippi also has a great culinary tradition. Being an agricultural state, many farms here produce fresh crops and livestock. From fresh seafood to farm raised catfish to fresh fruits and vegetables, Mississippi produces a great variety of foods. Some farms in Mississippi allow visitors to pick their own patches. Other farms sell their products at farmers markets and food festivals.

Mississippi has many boutique shops in historic districts and in outlet malls featuring nationally known brands. Jackson, Vicksburg, and Gulfport have major outlet malls. In addition, major nationally known stores can be found in Southaven, Tupelo, Meridian, Hattiesburg, and Biloxi. Over 50 cities in Mississippi are members of the Mississippi Main Street Association, which aims to help promote and revitalize downtown business districts.

The outdoors in Mississippi features great sportsman opportunities and includes some of the best hunting and fishing in the United States. Canoeing and kayaking is also popular in lakes and rivers in Mississippi. Hiking is popular in Mississippi and rock climbing is available at Tishomingo State Park in the northeast part of the state. Biking is also popular on the Natchez Trace Parkway, a scenic two lane highway extending from Natchez to Tishomingo County in Mississippi. Bird watching is common throughout the state, on the coast, and in state parks. Waterfalls can be found near Woodville in southwest Mississippi and at Tishomingo State Park.

Sporting events are very popular in Mississippi, particularly at the college and high school level. Football, baseball, and basketball are popular in the college towns in the state and at the many high schools in the state. Professional baseball can be found near Jackson in Pearl and near Biloxi while professional hockey can be found near Biloxi. Major championship golf courses are located throughout the state and some of them are designed by professional golfers. Many famous athletes are Mississippi natives including Jerry Rice, Brett Favre, Walter Payton, and many more.

Mississippi's colleges and universities include eight state supported institutions plus the University of Mississippi Medical Center. Three of the state supported universities are historically African-American institutions. Private colleges in Mississippi include Mississippi College, which is the oldest college in the state still in operation and is the largest private college in the state. Millsaps College and Belhaven College in Jackson along with William Carey University in Hattiesburg are also major private educational institutions in Mississippi. Blue Mountain College in north Mississippi has a long history dating over 140 years. Privately owned historically African American colleges in Mississippi include Tougaloo College in Jackson and Rust College in Holly Springs.

Major sites and battle fields of the American Civil War can be found in Mississippi. Major sites are located between Jackson, Vicksburg, and Natchez in southwest Mississippi and between Tupelo and Corinth in Northeast Mississippi. One of the most important battles of the Civil War occurred near Vicksburg and today visitors can learn more about the battle at Vicksburg National Military Park, which is one of the top tourist attractions in Mississippi. The Natchez Trace Parkway provides good access to these battlefields in southwest and northeast Mississippi.

Many antebellum homes were built in Mississippi after 1800 and prior to the Civil War (*antebellum* originates from Latin and means prewar). Many of these are available for tours or as bed and breakfast establishments. Antebellum homes commonly contain two or three floors, balconies, large porches, and Greek columns. A variety of architectural styles are seen in these homes and the most common is called Greek Revival style. Other styles include Classical Revival and Federal style. The largest and most elegant antebellum homes in Mississippi are located in Natchez, which has over 500 antebellum structures. Other destinations for antebellum homes in Mississippi include Vicksburg, Columbus, Aberdeen, Holly Springs, and Carrollton.

For art lovers, Jackson offers the state's largest art museum, the Mississippi Museum of Art. The coastal region also offers several quality art museums and Laurel has Mississippi's oldest art museum. Meridian has an impressive historic performing arts center that is one of the finest in the southeast United States. Other performing arts centers can be found in Jackson and Hattiesburg in addition to the campuses of Delta State University, the University of Mississippi in Oxford, and Mississippi State University in Starkville.

Mississippi has many great festivals that offer local cuisine, live music, amusement rides, and craft items for sale. Major festivals in Mississippi include the State Fair in Jackson, which is one of the largest in the state. Another large festival is the Neshoba County Fair, which is known for political speeches and horse racing. Other large festivals include the Mid-South Fair in Southaven, the Amory Railroad Festival, and the World Catfish Festival in Belzoni.

Many famous writers, musicians, and performers come from the Magnolia State. Mississippi's literary heritage includes many famous writers including William Faulkner, John Grisham, and Eudora Welty. Mississippi's musical heritage includes performers such as Elvis Presley, B.B. King, Jimmie Rodgers, Faith Hill, and many more. Famous actors and television personalities from Mississippi include Morgan Freeman, Oprah Winfrey, Sela Ward, Robin Roberts, and many more.

Mississippi's diverse heritage includes European American, African American, and Native American culture. In 2017, Mississippi will open the first Civil Rights Museum in downtown Jackson to honor the struggles of African Americans and other ethnicities throughout the state's history. Native American heritage can be explored in Neshoba County, where the largest numbers of remaining Choctaw Native Americans in Mississippi live. The Choctaw are the only recognized

Native American tribe in Mississippi. Native American burial mounds can be found at locations including Natchez, Belzoni, Greenville, and near Neshoba County. Some of these mounds are close to 2,000 years old.

So if one takes the time to explore Mississippi, a diverse selection of natural and cultural attractions can be found. Mississippi is a beautiful state and its people make the state even better. Mississippi offers almost everything that other states offer in terms of tourism plus many unique attractions. So whether you are a native Mississippian or a first time visitor, come home to Mississippi and see what you have been missing.

GETTING TO MISSISSIPPI

Mississippi's largest airport is the **Jackson-Evers International Airport**, which has flights from Atlanta, Dallas, Chicago, Houston, Charlotte, and Washington D.C. Jackson-Evers would be a good choice for those wanting to explore Mississippi's historical attractions in central and southwest Mississippi. Jackson-Evers is also within driving distance to the Delta region, Meridian, Philadelphia, and Hattiesburg.

Gulfport-Biloxi International Airport has flights from Atlanta, Dallas, St. Petersburg, Houston, and Charlotte. For those wanting to explore the Mississippi coastal region and south Mississippi, Gulfport-Biloxi is a good choice.

Memphis International Airport has a large selection of flights from across the United States and is a good option for those wanting to explore the Delta and Hills regions of North Mississippi including Tunica, Clarksdale, Oxford, and Tupelo.

For those travelling to Mississippi by car, most places in the state are accessible by an interstate or a four-lane highway. The scenic **Natchez Trace Parkway** runs from southwest Mississippi in Natchez through Jackson and Tupelo until crossing into Alabama. **Interstate 20** runs west-east and connects Vicksburg and Jackson to Meridian. **Interstate 55** runs north-south and connects Memphis and North Mississippi with Jackson and South Mississippi. **Interstate 59** connects Meridian to Laurel, Hattiesburg, Picayune, and New Orleans. **Interstate 10** runs west-east and connects Biloxi and Gulfport with New Orleans and Mobile. Other highways include **Highway 61**, which runs north-south from Memphis through Tunica, Clarksdale, Cleveland, Vicksburg, Natchez, and Woodville. Scenic **Highway 90** runs parallel to Interstate 10 on the Mississippi coast.

Since many attractions in Mississippi are spread out in towns across the state, having access to an automobile is essential. Rental cars are available for those who fly into the state or for those who do not have an automobile.

MISSISSIPPI HISTORY

Prior to European settlement, the land included in present day Mississippi was inhabited by Native American tribes. The most prominent of which were the Choctaw, Chickasaw, and Natchez Indians.

Spanish explorer Hernando DeSoto entered Mississippi in 1541 just south of present day Memphis on the Mississippi River. Desoto became the first known European to enter present day Mississippi.

In 1673, French missionary Jacques Marquette and French Canadian explorer Louis Jolliet explored the Mississippi River. After entering present day Mississippi, they reached as far downstream as present day Rosedale before turning back.

FRENCH RULE

In 1682, Robert Cavalier de La Salle explored the Mississippi River to its mouth and claimed all lands drained by the river for France.

In 1699, several Frenchmen founded the first European settlement in present day Mississippi. The settlement was called Fort Maurepas (also called Old Biloxi) and was located on the site of the present day city of Ocean Springs, Mississippi. The Frenchmen included Pierre Le Moyne d'Iberville and his brother, Jean Baptiste Le Moyne, Sieur de Bienville.

Fort Rosalie was established by the French on the present day city of Natchez, Mississippi in 1716.

French settlers at Fort Rosalie were attacked and massacred by the Natchez Indians in 1729. Three years later in 1732, the French retaliated and attacked the Natchez Indians with help from the Choctaw Indians. As a result of this retaliation, the Natchez Indians were destroyed and ceased to exist as a tribe.

BRITISH RULE

After the French and Indian War in 1763, Mississippi and all French territory east of the Mississippi River passed into English control.

SPANISH RULE

In 1779, Governor of Spanish Louisiana Bernardo Galvez captured and gained control of Natchez.

The Treaty of Paris in 1781 gave Spain the southern half of present day Mississippi while America gained the northern half of the present state.

UNITED STATES

The United States gained control of Natchez in 1797 and all land in Mississippi north of the 31st parallel.

Mississippi officially became an American Territory in 1798.

The Treaty of Mount Dexter in 1805 gave the U.S. more territory by exchanging debts owed by Native Americans.

In 1812, Mississippi's boundary east of the Pearl River was extended south to the Gulf of Mexico.

The Treaty of Fort Stephens with the Choctaw Indians in 1816 opened three million acres of land for settlement.

Mississippi became the 20th state of the United States in 1817.

Andrew Jackson and Thomas Hinds negotiated the Treaty of Doak's Stand in 1820, giving the United States five million acres of land that once belonged to the Choctaw Indians.

The state capital was moved to Jackson in 1822 and was named after Major General Andrew Jackson.

The Treaty of Dancing Rabbit Creek ceded all Choctaw territory east of the Mississippi River to the United States in 1830 and most Choctaws left the state for Oklahoma.

The Treaty of Pontotoc ceded all Chickasaw land east of the Mississippi River to the United States in 1832 and the Chickasaws left the state for Oklahoma.

CIVIL WAR

In 1861, Mississippi seceded from the United States along with several other states to preserve slavery.

Many battles were fought between 1861 and 1865 in Mississippi and the United States. The war was the bloodiest in America's history. Many cities in Mississippi were severely damaged including Jackson.

The Civil War was devastating for Mississippi, but the state eventually recovered and was officially readmitted to the United States in 1870.

POST WAR

Construction of railroads in the 1870's helped towns in Mississippi recover from the Civil War. Many towns in Mississippi grew rapidly in the late 19th century and early 20th century.

Mississippi legislators created a new State Constitution in 1890 and this document is still in use today.

THE 20TH CENTURY

The Mississippi River flooded about three million acres of land in the Delta Region in 1927. The Great Mississippi Flood of 1927 was the worst flood in Mississippi history.

Oil was discovered in Mississippi in 1939 in Yazoo County, which is about 40 miles northwest of Jackson.

The World War II period of the early 1940's created an industrial boom in Mississippi and across the United States.

The United States Supreme Court decision in 1954 led to the desegregation of schools and marked the beginning of the Civil Rights Movement.

James Meredith entered the University of Mississippi in 1962 as the first African American student amid violent riots and national headlines.

The Civil Rights Movement continues during the 1960's as public places became desegregated and voting rights for African Americans were established.

Civil Rights activist and NAACP field secretary Medgar Evers was assassinated in 1963, which made national headlines and strengthened the Civil Rights Movement as many marched in protest during the funeral.

The United States Congress passed the Civil Rights Act in 1964, which outlawed segregation in public places.

Hurricane Camille caused major destruction on the Mississippi Coast in 1969. Another devastating storm came in 2005 as Hurricane Katrina caused major destruction to the Mississippi Coast and New Orleans.

Mississippi hosted the International Ballet Competition for the first time in 1982 in downtown Jackson's Thalia Mara Hall.

The first auto assembly plant opened in Mississippi as Nissan built a plant in Canton in 2003. In 2011, Toyota built an assembly plant in Blue Springs near Tupelo.

FAMOUS MISSISSIPPIANS

Mississippi has produced many famous authors, musicians, artists, and actors including:

Elvis Presley, musician

John Grisham, author

Faith Hill, musician

Morgan Freeman, actor

Oprah Winfrey, television personality

Jim Henson, creator of the *Muppets*

Sela Ward, actress

B.B. King, musician

Marty Stuart, musician

William Faulkner, author

Robin Roberts, television personality

Jimmy Buffet, musician

Eudora Welty, author

Bo Diddley, musician

Jimmie Rodgers, musician

TOP FESTIVALS IN MISSISSIPPI

HISTORIC TRIANGLE REGION

Jackson

Mississippi State Fair, Jackson, October

Dixie National Livestock Show and Rodeo, Jackson, January, February

Mississippi Blues Marathon and Half-Marathon, Jackson, January.

Mal's St. Paddy's Day Parade, Jackson, March

Canton

Canton Flea Market Arts and Crafts Show, May, October

Vicksburg

Tapestry: The Pilgrimage to Vicksburg, April

Riverfest Music and Arts Festival, Vicksburg, April

Vicksburg Fall Fest, October

Natchez

Natchez Spring Pilgrimage, March, September

Natchez Festival of Music, May

Natchez Powwow, March

Natchez Food and Wine Festival, July

Brookhaven

Ole Brook Festival, September

SOUTHEAST MISSISSIPPI REGION

Hattiesburg

Hubfest, Hattiesburg, March

FestivalSouth, Hattiesburg, June

Collins

Okatoma Festival, Collins, May

Mitchell Farms Pumpkin Patch, Collins, October

Mississippi Peanut Festival, Mitchell Farms, Collins, October

Laurel

Lauren Rodgers Museum of Art Blues Bash, Laurel, June

South Mississippi Fair, Laurel, October

COASTAL REGION OF MISSISSIPPI

Biloxi

Coliseum Crawfish Music Festival, Biloxi, April

Biloxi Seafood Festival, Biloxi, September

Crusin' the Coast, Biloxi, October

Biloxi St. Patrick's Day Parade and Grillin' on the Green, March

The Mississippi Gulf Coast Carnival Association Mardi Gras Parade, Biloxi, March

Coast Coliseum Summer Fair, Biloxi, June

Gulfport

Gulf Coast Yacht and Boat Super Show, Gulfport, April

Gulfport Music Festival, May

Pass Christian

Pass Christian Oyster Festival, January

Mississippi Gulf Coast Spring Pilgrimage, Pass Christian, March

Art in the Pass, Pass Christian, April

Christmas in the Pass, Pass Christian, December

Bay St. Louis

Bay BridgeFest, Bay St. Louis, September

Waveland

WaveFest, Waveland, October

Long Beach

Mississippi Gulf Coast Kite Festival, Long Beach, April

Pascagoula

Live Oak Arts Festival, Pascagoula, May

Zonta Arts & Crafts Festival, Pascagoula, October

Jackson County Fair, Pascagoula, October

Mississippi Gulf Coast Blues & Heritage Festival, Pascagoula, September

Ocean Springs

Peter Anderson Arts and Crafts Festival, Ocean Springs, November

DELTA REGION OF NORTHWEST MISSISSIPPI

Greenville

Delta Blues Festival, Greenville, September

Hot Tamale Festival, Greenville, October

Highway 61 Blues Festival and Mighty Mississippi Music Festival, Greenville, October

Clarksdale

Mississippi Delta Tennessee Williams Festival, Clarksdale, October

Pinetop Perkins Homecoming, Clarksdale, October

Cleveland

Octoberfest, Cleveland, October

Indianola

B.B. King Homecoming Festival, Indianola

Belzoni

World Catfish Festival, Belzoni, April

Greenwood

River to the Rails Festival, Greenwood, May

Carrollton

Historic Pilgrimage, Carrollton, October

Yazoo City

Jerry Clower Festival, Yazoo City, May

THE HILLS OF NORTH MISSISSIPPI REGION

Southaven

Crystal Ball, Southaven, January

Mid-South Fair, Southaven, September

Holly Springs

Holly Springs Pilgrimage, April

Oxford

Oxford Film Festival, February

Double Decker Arts Festival, April

Tupelo

Tupelo Elvis Festival, June

Tupelo Film Festival, April

Gumtree Arts Festival, Tupelo, May

Corinth

Slugburger Festival, Corinth, July

Grenada

Thunder on the Water Festival, Grenada, June

Balloons over Grenada, August

PINES REGION OF EAST MISSISSIPPI

Amory

Amory Railroad Festival, Amory, April

Starkville

Magnolia Independent Film Festival, Starkville, February

Cotton District Arts Festival, Starkville, April

West Point

Prairie Arts Festival, West Point, August

Aberdeen

Southern Heritage Pilgrimage, Aberdeen, April

Kosciusko

Natchez Trace Festival, Kosciusko, April

Central Mississippi Fair, Kosciusko, August

Columbus

Spring Pilgrimage, Columbus, April

Market Street Festival, Columbus, May

Tennessee Williams Tribute, Columbus, September

Meridian

Threefoot Arts Festival, Meridian, April

Jimmie Rodgers Festival, Meridian, May

State Games of Mississippi, Meridian, June

Neshoba County

Choctaw Indian Fair, Neshoba County, July

Neshoba County Fair, Philadelphia, July, August

Vardaman

Vardaman Sweet Potato Festival, Vardaman, November

THE HISTORIC TRIANGLE REGION OF SOUTHWEST MISSISSIPPI

The Historic Triangle of Southwest Mississippi includes Natchez, Vicksburg, and Jackson as the top attractions. Other destinations in the Historic Triangle include Port Gibson and Woodville. Visitors can access the Historic Triangle by air from the Jackson-Evers International Airport. Interstate 20 runs east-west through Jackson, Vicksburg, and Meridian. Interstate 55 runs north-south from Memphis to Jackson and south Mississippi. Highway 49 is a four-lane highway running from northwest Mississippi through Jackson and southeast Mississippi. The scenic Natchez Trace Parkway runs from Natchez through Jackson to Tupelo and the state line. Highway 61 is a four-lane highway (in most sections) running north-south and connects Vicksburg, Natchez, and Woodville to Greenville and northwest Mississippi.

JACKSON

Jackson-Evers International Airport provides access to Jackson from several cities across the United States. Interstate highways 20 and 55 also provide access to Jackson from all four directions. Highway 49 connects Jackson with northwest and southeast Mississippi. The Natchez Trace Parkway connects Jackson to southwest and northeast Mississippi. Highway 25 also connects Jackson to northeast Mississippi. Information and maps can be found at the **Jackson Convention and Visitors Bureau** at 111 East Capitol Street. Contact (800) 354-7695 or (601) 960-1891.

HISTORY

The area now known as Jackson was originally inhabited by Native Americans of the Choctaw Tribe. The Treaty of Doak's Stand with the United States Government and the Choctaw opened up land in present day central Mississippi for European settlement in 1820. Jackson was founded in 1821 at a trading post on a tall bluff on the west bank of the Pearl River. The town was originally called LeFleur's Bluff and was named after a French-Canadian trader. The Mississippi State Legislature wanted a more central location for the State Capital and decided to move the Capital to LeFleur's Bluff in 1821.

The town was renamed Jackson after Major General Andrew Jackson (who would later become President of the United States). A small two-story brick building was built in 1822 for the capitol, but when Jackson was authorized by the state legislature to be the permanent capital in 1832, authorization was given to build a much larger building. In 1839, a large Greek Revival style building was built in Jackson as the permanent **capitol building** and served the city and state for many years through important events including the Civil War period. A newer, larger Capitol was built in 1903 while the previous capitol building is now a museum. The **Governor's Mansion** was authorized to be built in 1839 and was completed in 1842. The mansion is the oldest residence of its type in the nation. The beautiful three-story **Jackson City Hall** was built in 1846 and continues to serve the city today. Jackson did not grow much in the 1800's and the Civil War period was devastating. During the war, Jackson was ravaged and burned three times by Union troops under the command of General William Tecumseh Sherman. Somehow, City Hall survived the burning (most likely because it was used as a hospital). The Old Capitol building also survived the war.

In 1900, Jackson only had 8,000 residents but the city began to increase rapidly in population. Railroads helped spur new growth and several large buildings were built in downtown Jackson. The discovery of natural gas near Jackson was also a boost to the economy and helped offset the effects of the Great Depression of the 1930's. During World War II, Hawkins Field in northwest Jackson was developed as a major airbase. Jackson's population increased from 8,000 in 1900 to 21,000 in 1910; 48,000 in 1930, 62,000 in 1940, 98,000 in 1950, and 144,000 in 1960. By 1980, Jackson had over 200,000 residents in its city limits.

The Civil Rights movement became more active in the city by 1950. In the 1960's, dramatic non-violent protests and demonstrations occurred. Jackson was segregated and Jim Crow laws were still in effect. In 1963, civil rights activist **Medgar Evers** was murdered and thousands of people marched at his funeral procession to protest the killing. The Civil Rights Act of 1964 and the Voting Rights Act of 1965 gradually helped end segregation and disenfranchisement of African Americans in Jackson and Mississippi.

Jackson continued to grow economically in the late 20th century. New commercial buildings and government offices were constructed in downtown Jackson. The **University of Mississippi Medical Center** has grown dramatically in addition to Jackson State University, private

Millsaps College, and Belhaven College. **Jackson-Evers International Airport** has seen significant growth and a new convention center in downtown Jackson in 2009 has helped revitalize the downtown area.

HISTORICAL ATTRACTIONS

Jackson City Hall, the Old Capitol Museum, and the Governor's mansion were the few surviving buildings in Jackson after the Civil War. The **Old Capitol Museum** is located inside the Old Capitol Building, which was built in 1839 in the Greek Revival style and was designed by William Nichols. Many historic events occurred at the Capitol including visits by Andrew Jackson, Henry Clay, and Jefferson Davis. In the House of Representatives on January 9, 1861, Mississippi became an independent republic and the second state to secede from the United States. The 1890 Mississippi Constitution, under which Mississippi is still governed, was adopted in the building. The new Capitol was built in 1903 and the Old Capitol became an office building. In 1961, the Old Capitol became the State Historical Museum and continues to this day. A major renovation of the museum was completed in 2009. The museum is located at 100 South State Street and admission is free. Tours are also available by reservation. Hours: Tues-Sat 9-5 P.M., Sun 1-5 P.M. Contact (601) 576-6920.

The **Mississippi Governor's Mansion** was built in 1842 in the Greek Revival style. Designed by William Nichols, the mansion is the second oldest continuously occupied governor's residence in the United States and was designated a National Historic Landmark in 1975. Tours of the mansion are available and admission is free. Hours: Tues-Fri 9:30-11 A.M. Contact (601) 359-6421. **Jackson City Hall** was completed in 1847 and served as a hospital for both Union and Confederate forces in the Civil War. The beautiful Greek Revival style building is a popular landmark in the city of Jackson. Jackson City Hall is located at 219 South President Street and free tours are available. Contact (601) 960-1111.

One of the most impressive buildings in Jackson is the current **State Capitol** building, which was built in 1903 with the Beaux-Arts style. The building stands 180 feet tall and 402 feet wide. A large dome is at the top center with two wings on each side consisting of four floors. On top of the dome is an 8 foot tall and 15 foot wide copper statue of an eagle. The Capitol is located at 400 High Street and free tours are available. Contact (601) 359-3114. Tours are given weekdays 9:30-11 A.M. and 1-2:30 P.M.

Soldiers of all wars are remembered at the **War Memorial Building** at 120 North State Street, where faces of soldiers are carved into the building. **Greenwood Cemetery** is one of the oldest cemeteries in the city and is the burial place of Eudora Welty, war generals, soldiers, and past governors of Mississippi. Greenwood Cemetery is located at West Street and Lamar Street.

HISTORIC HOMES

A few antebellum homes remain in Jackson. The **Cedars House** was built around 1840 and is Jackson's oldest residential home. Located on a two acre property, the one story home hosts weddings, receptions, cultural and community events. The home has been restored and preserved by the Fondren Renaissance Foundation and is located at 4145 Old Canton Road. Contact (601) 366-5552. The **Oaks House** is one of Jackson's oldest homes and is described as a Greek Revival style cottage. Built in 1853 on four acres of land, the Oaks was the home of the Boyd family. James Boyd was a long time mayor and alderman of Jackson. The Oaks House can be found at 823 North Jefferson Street and admission is required. Contact (601) 353-9339. The last tour begins at 2:15 P.M. The **Manship House** is a Gothic Revival style home of Civil War era Jackson mayor Charles Manship. Built in 1857, the home began a major restoration project in 2010 by the Mississippi Department of Archives and History. The Manship House can be found at 420 East Fortification Street. Contact (601) 961-4724.

The **Eudora Welty House** was the residence of Pulitzer Prize winning author Eudora Welty (1908-2001) for 76 years. Welty completed her writings in the home, which is one of the most authentic literary homes in America in terms of original furnishings. This National Historic Landmark is located in the Belhaven neighborhood and includes a garden. The home was restored by the Mississippi Department of Archives and History in 2001 and is open for tours. The home is located at 1119 Pinehurst Street and admission is required. Hours: Tue.-Fri. 9-11 A.M., 1-3 P.M. Contact (601) 353-7762.

The **Medgar Evers House** is the family home of Medgar Evers, a civil rights activist who was murdered at his home by a white supremacist, Byron De La Beckwith in June 1963. Evers was a field secretary for the NAACP and worked for equal rights for all people. Tours of the home are by appointment only and admission is free. The home is located at 2332 Margaret Walker Alexander Drive. Contact (601) 977-7839 or (601) 977-7842. The **Medgar Evers Library** is a city owned library near the Evers home and features exhibits and information about Medgar Evers, including a life-size bronze statue. The library is located at 4215 Medgar Evers Boulevard. Hours: Mon.-Thu. 9-7 P.M., Fri.-Sat. 9-5 P.M. Contact (601) 982-2867.

HISTORIC BUILDINGS AND DISTRICTS

Downtown Jackson saw several large buildings constructed during a building boom in the 1920's. The **King Edward Hotel** was a 12 story Beaux Arts style hotel built in 1923. After being vacant for 40 years, a major renovation began in 2007 and was completed in 2009. A Hilton Garden Inn was created inside the upscale hotel, which features 186 rooms, 64 luxury apartments, a restaurant, and retail space at 235 West Capitol Street. Contact (601) 353-5464. The **Lamar Life** building was built in 1924 and was considered Jackson's first skyscraper. The 10 story landmark building features Neo-Gothic architecture including a clock tower. Several other large buildings were built in the 1920's. The **Standard Life Building** is another landmark building which was built in 1929. The 22 story art-deco style building was renovated in 2010 into apartments. The 18 story **Regions Bank Building** was also built in 1929 in the Renaissance Revival style. Many modern buildings also shape the Jackson skyline today.

The **Alamo Theater** is located in the Farish Street Historic District and has hosted live performing arts since 1942. The Alamo has hosted performances by B.B. King, Nat King Cole, and Dorothy Moore. The 525 seat theater hosts movies, music competitions, blues and jazz concerts, gospel and vocal ensembles. The non-profit theater is located at 333 North Farish Street. Contact (601) 352-3365. The **Smith Robertson Museum** focuses on the contributions of African Americans including art, photography, work, lifestyle, and an understanding of the African American experience in the deep South. The museum is known for having a large collection of quilts and is housed in a building which served as the first public school (1894) for African American children in Jackson. The museum is located at 528 Bloom Street and is within walking distance of the State Capitol building. Admission is required at the museum. Hours: Mon-Fri 9-5 P.M. and Sat 10-1 P.M. Contact (601) 960-1457.

Tougaloo College was founded in 1869 as a historically black private liberal arts college and is located at 500 West County Line Road. The college had a vital role in the Civil Rights movement of the 1960's and houses photographs, artifacts, and documents from the movement at Coleman Library. Hours: Mon-Thurs 8 A.M- 11 P.M., Fri 8-5 P.M., Sat 12-4 P.M., Sun 3-9 P.M. Contact (601) 977-7700.

The **Fondren Historic District** was one of the first suburban neighborhoods in Jackson to have a business district and today features shops, great restaurants, notable art galleries, eclectic architecture, and charming homes. Located northeast of downtown Jackson, the district is bordered by Northside Drive, Woodrow Wilson Street, and Mill Street. The Fondren district also includes four hospitals and the University of Mississippi Medical Center. Bordering Fondren to the south is the **Belhaven** neighborhood, which features historic residential homes, Belhaven University, Millsaps College, shops, restaurants, a theater, and a bed and breakfast.

THE ARTS IN JACKSON

Jackson features Mississippi's largest art museum, the **Mississippi Museum of Art**. With a collection of over 4,000 works, the museum focuses on Mississippi artists in its permanent collection and changing exhibitions but also has a large collection of American art. The museum also features an art garden, restaurant, and museum store. In 2007, a major renovation of the museum was completed in a new location. The art garden was completed in 2011 and features a 1.2 acre public green space with outdoor art. The museum is located at 380 South Lamar Street in downtown Jackson. Admission is required for some exhibitions but otherwise is free. Hours: Tue.-Sat. 10-5 P.M. and Sun. 12-5 P.M. Contact (601) 960-1515.

Jackson has been host of the **USA International Ballet Competition** every four years since 1982 and most recently was held in 2014 in downtown Jackson. The two-week Olympic style competition features competitors from around the world and was founded by Thalia Mara in 1978. In 1982, the United States Congress named Jackson, Mississippi host of the USA International Ballet Competition. Thalia Mara Hall is located at 255 East Pascagoula Street. Contact (601) 960-1537.

Ballet Mississippi is one of the top performing arts organizations in the region and originated in 1964. Ballet Mississippi offers performances throughout the year for the public to enjoy, including the *Nutcracker* each December at Thalia Mara Hall. In addition to performances, Ballet Mississippi offers a pre-professional ballet school that focuses on classical ballet technique and trains a variety of ages including children and adults. Ballet Mississippi is located at 201 East Pascagoula Street. Contact (601) 960-1560 for ticket information.

The **Mississippi Opera** was founded in 1945 and is the 10th oldest opera company in the nation. Mississippi Opera produces high quality productions that have received great reviews from the region and nationally. A variety of performances are offered during the year. The Mississippi Opera is located at the Mississippi Arts Center at 201 East Pascagoula Street. Contact (601) 960-2300 for ticket information.

New Stage Theatre was founded in 1965 and is Mississippi's only professional theater. New Stage Theater produces live on stage performances including Broadway style plays and musicals. The theater produces a full season of shows from September to June and is located at 1100 Carlisle Street. Contact (601) 948-3533 for ticket information.

Just north of Jackson is the **Mississippi Crafts Center** in Ridgeland. Since 1973, the Craftsmen's Guild of Mississippi has preserved, promoted, and marketed regional crafts and today has a membership of over 400 professional artisans from across the Southeast United States. The current center is a state of the art facility opened in 2007 and features fine craft, traditional and contemporary folk art, live demonstrations, and special events. The center is located at 950 Rice Road in Ridgeland and can be reached from the Natchez Trace Parkway. Hours: 9-5 P.M. Mon-Sun. Contact (601) 856-7546.

RECREATION AND CHILDREN

One of the most popular attractions in Jackson for children and adults, the **Mississippi Museum of Natural Science** focuses on Mississippi's biological diversity through collections, research, education, and exhibits. Located inside LeFleur's Bluff State Park, the 73,000 foot facility is located on a 300 acre natural landscape and features 2.5 miles of nature trails, wooden boardwalks, and an open-air amphitheater. Inside the museum is a 100, 000 gallon aquarium housing over 200 living species of native fish, reptiles, and amphibians, a 1,700 square foot greenhouse, a variety of exhibits, a gift shop, library, and theater. The museum is located at 2148 Riverside Drive and admission is required. Hours: Mon.-Fri. 8-5 P.M., Sat 9-5 P.M., Sun 1-5 P.M. Contact (601) 576-6000.

The **Mississippi Children's Museum** focuses on hands-on exhibits and programs focusing on cultural arts, science, and technology, literacy, health, nutrition, and Mississippi heritage. The museum is one of the top children's attractions in Jackson and receives great reviews. The 40,000 square foot museum is located at 2145 Highland Drive and admission is required. Hours: Tue.-Sat. 9-5 P.M., Sun. 1-6 P.M. Contact (601) 981-5469.

The **Russell C. Davis Planetarium** features one of the South's largest planetariums. The hemisphere shaped, 60 foot diameter dome planetarium uses an advanced digital projection system to produce astronomy shows and large format films. Scenes of stars, planets, and celestial objects appear on the dome and simulate the motions of the heavens. The planetarium is located at 201 East Pascagoula Street and admission is charged. Contact (601) 960-1550 for show times.

The **Jackson Zoo** is a popular attraction for children and families and is the largest zoo in Mississippi in terms of number and diversity of exotic species. Located inside the historic 110 acre Livingston Park, the zoo contains about 800 animals from over 120 species. Animal habitats featured in the zoo include the African rainforest, the African savannah, Mississippi Wilderness, South America, and Asia. The zoo is located at 2918 West Capitol Street and admission is required. Hours: Mon.-Sun. 9-4 P.M. Contact (601) 352-2580.

Mynelle Gardens is the most recognized botanical garden in the area. The gardens are landscaped with sidewalks and feature azalea and camellia trails, daylily displays, perennials, and annuals along with song birds. A gift shop is available at the gardens. The gardens are located at 4736 Clinton Boulevard and admission is required. Hours: Mon.-Sun. 9-5 P.M. (Mar-Oct), Mon.-Sat. 8-4 P.M. (Nov-Feb). Contact (601) 960-1894.

The **Mississippi Sports Hall of Fame** features a variety of sports interactive exhibits focused on accomplished athletes and teams from the state of Mississippi from high school to professional level. Digital exhibits allow visitors to access archival footage, data and information, and interviews from athletes such as Jerry Rice, Brett Favre, Archie Manning, and Dizzy Dean. The Museum can be located at 1152 Lakeland Drive and admission is required. Hours: Mon.-Sat. 10-4 P.M. Contact (601) 982-8264.

Trustmark Park is the home of the Mississippi Braves minor league baseball team. Opening in 2005, the park holds over 8,000 fans on two levels with luxury seats on the second level. The park is located east of Jackson in Pearl near Bass Pro Drive.

SHOPPING

The **Outlets of Mississippi** is the largest outlet shopping center in Mississippi and offers nationally known clothing brands at discounted prices. The 325,000 square foot center is located at 200 Bass Pro Drive in Pearl. Hours: Mon.-Sat. 10 A.M.-9 P.M., Sun. 12-7 P.M. Contact (769) 972-3000.

Renaissance at Colony Park is a world class lifestyle shopping destination with classic architectural design and features nationally known stores, restaurants, and an upscale hotel. Renaissance is located at 1000 Highland Colony Parkway in Ridgeland (just north of Jackson). Hours: Mon.-Thu. 10-7 P.M., Fri-Sat 10-8 P.M., Sun 1-6 P.M. Contact (601) 519-0900.

The **Antique Mall of the South** is the largest antique mall in central Mississippi and features a variety of antiques including furniture, glassware, and collectibles. The mall is located at 367 Highway 51 in Ridgeland. Hours: Mon.-Sat. 10-6 P.M., Sun. 1-6 P.M. Contact (601) 853-4000.

DINING IN JACKSON

Babalu Tacos and Tapas is located at 622 Duling Avenue near the Fondren District. Contact (601) 366-5757. Hours: Mon.-Thu. 11-10 P.M., Fri.-Sat. 11-11 P.M., Sun. 11-9 P.M.

Bravo! Italian Restaurant is located at 4500 Interstate 55 Frontage Road and Northside Drive (Highland Village). Contact (601) 982-8111. Hours: Tue.-Sat. 11-10 P.M., Sun. 11-9 P.M.

Char (Steaks) is located at 4500 Interstate 55 North and Northside Drive (Highland Village). Contact (601) 956-9562. Hours: Mon.-Thu. 11-10 P.M., Fri.-Sat. 11-10:30, Sun. 10-9.

Keifer's Restaurant serves Greek cuisine and is located at 120 North Congress Street in downtown Jackson. Contact (601) 353-4976. Hours: Mon.-Fri. 11-2:30 P.M.

Walker's is located at 3016 North State Street in the Fondren District. Contact (601) 982-2633. Hours: 11-2 P.M. Mon.-Fri. (lunch), 5:30 P.M. (dinner).

FESTIVALS AND EVENTS

The **Mississippi State Fair** is one of the largest fairs in the South and is held annually in early October at the State Fairgrounds in Jackson. The two-week fair offers amusement rides, concessions, music, entertainment, and agricultural and livestock competition. Contact (601) 961-4000.

The **Dixie National Livestock Show and Rodeo** in Jackson is one of the largest of its type in the eastern United States and is held annually in late January to early February at the Mississippi State Fairgrounds. In addition to rodeo, the three-week event hosts horse shows, livestock shows, festivals, trade shows, and a parade. Contact (601) 961-4000.

Mal's St. Paddy's Day Parade is held in downtown Jackson for a weekend in late March. The parade attracts thousands of participants from around the world and also features a festival with music, a ball, parties, running contests, and children's activities. Contact (800) 354-7695.

The **Mississippi Blues Marathon and Half-Marathon** is held in Jackson in January and is sponsored by Blue Cross and Blue Shield of Mississippi. The marathon hosts competitors from around the world and also offers food and blues music. Contact (601) 624-7882.

STAYING SAFE

Jackson is a large city and is known to have crime issues, particularly in west and south Jackson. The downtown business district is relatively safe during business hours, in addition to northeast Jackson, Fondren, and Belhaven neighborhood. A good idea is to avoid gas stations and convenience stores in Jackson, particularly in west and south Jackson and during evening hours. Use caution when visiting the Jackson Zoo and Mynelle Gardens in West Jackson.

CANTON AND MADISON COUNTY

Madison County was created in 1828 and was named after President James Madison. Located 26 miles north of Jackson, the **Madison County Courthouse** (1858) is a beautiful two-story Greek Revival style building surrounded by green space and a town square. The courthouse can be found at Liberty Street in Canton. The courthouse square is the site of the nationally recognized **Canton Flea Market and Arts & Crafts Show**, which is held twice per year. Sites in Canton have been featured in five major Hollywood films, including the Madison County Courthouse. Today, Canton is home to the **Mississippi Film Studios**, a 31 acre site that includes a 36,000 square foot facility and office space. Canton is also home to the **Nissan Automotive Assembly Plant**. The **Canton Convention and Visitors Bureau** is located at 147 North Union Street. Hours: Mon.-Fri. 10-5 P.M., Sat. 10-2 P.M. Contact (601) 859-1307.

The **Canton Flea Market Arts and Crafts Show** attracts up to 1,000 artisans from across the United States who showcase their handmade pottery, jewelry, arts and crafts. Began in 1965, the show is held in May and October annually on the lawn of the Historic Madison County Courthouse. Contact (601) 859-1307.

The Chapel of the Cross is a Gothic style chapel built in 1850 for the Episcopal Church congregation in Madison. A historic cemetery lies behind the chapel along with a rectory, Parish Hall, and education buildings. The chapel is located at 674 Mannsdale Road (just north of Jackson and Ridgeland). Contact (601) 856-2593.

The **Natchez Trace Visitor Center** near Ridgeland can be found at milepost 102.4. The **Ross Barnet Reservoir** can be also found by way of the Natchez Trace Parkway in Ridgeland. Named for former Governor Ross Barnett, the 33,000 acre reservoir was formed by impounding the Pearl River between Madison and Rankin County. Completed in 1965, the Reservoir has 105 miles of shoreline for activities such as boating, sailing, watersports, camping, fishing, and bird watching. Contact: (601) 856-6574.

CLINTON

Founded in 1823 and located just west of Jackson, Clinton was originally known as Mount Salus, which was the name of the Clinton home of the third governor of Mississippi Walter Leake. In 1828, the town name was changed to Clinton in honor of DeWitt Clinton, a former New York governor. The **Clinton Visitor Center** is located just off the Natchez Trace at 1300 Pinehaven Road. Contact: (601) 924-2221.

Mississippi College was established in 1826 and is the oldest operating college in Mississippi. The college is also the second oldest Baptist college in the world. Near College and Jefferson Street is the Clinton historic downtown (known as "**Olde Towne**") and features brick streets, shops, and cafes. Other historical attractions include **Provine Chapel** (1860) which is located at 200 West College Street. **Clinton Cemetery** (1800) is one of the oldest cemeteries in Mississippi and is located at 500 College Street.

RAYMOND

Raymond is located southwest of Jackson and shares the county seat of Hinds County with Jackson. Founded in 1828, Raymond is also located near the Natchez Trace Parkway. The **Battle of Raymond** was fought between Union and Confederate soldiers as part of General Ulysses S. Grant's Vicksburg Campaign in 1863 and Grant's Union forces were victorious. Main Street in Raymond has several historic buildings, including several churches. **Hinds County Courthouse** was completed in 1859 using the Greek Revival style and is located at 127 Main Street. **Saint Mark's Episcopal Church** dates back to 1854 and served as a Union hospital during the Battle of Raymond. Located at 205 West Main Street, blood stains can still be seen in the church from the battle. Raymond is also the home of Hinds Community College, the largest college in Mississippi. The **Raymond Chamber of Commerce** is located at 104 North Oak Street. Contact: (601) 857-8942.

VICKSBURG

Vicksburg is located 44 miles west of Jackson on Interstate 20. Highway 61 provides access to Vicksburg from Greenville and Natchez.

HISTORY

French colonists were the first European settlers in the Vicksburg area, establishing Fort-Saint-Pierre in 1719 at Redwood just north of Vicksburg. The Natchez and Choctaw Indians were eventually driven out of the area by the early 1800's. When Spain took control of the settlement, a military outpost called Fort Nogales was established. When the United States gained possession of the settlement in 1798, the name was changed to Walnut Hills. In 1825, the settlement had grown into a village and was incorporated as Vicksburg after Newitt Vick, a Methodist minister who established a mission on the site.

During the Civil War, Vicksburg eventually surrendered during the Seige of Vicksburg when the Union Army gained control of the entire Mississippi River. The 47-day siege was intended to starve the city into submission since its location on top of a high bluff overlooking the Mississippi River shielded attacks from Union forces. The surrender of Vicksburg by Confederate General John C. Pemberton on July 4, 1863 along with the defeat of General Robert E. Lee at Gettysburg, Pennsylvania the day before has historically marked the turning point in the Civil War in the Union's favor.

In the 1800's Vicksburg had a strong economy because of steam boat traffic on the Mississippi River, shipping cotton and other goods. Vicksburg had a population of over 20,000 by 1910. In 1876, a Mississippi River flood cut off a large meander channel flowing past Vicksburg, which left limited access to the new channel. This caused the economy of Vicksburg to suffer greatly.

By the early 1900's improvements in transportation infrastructure allowed a boost to the economy of Vicksburg. In 1903, the United States Army Corps of Engineers was successful in diverting the Yazoo River into the old, shallowing channel to rejuvenate the waterfront of Vicksburg. Railroad access to the west was available by transfer steamers and ferry barges until a combination railroad and highway bridge was built in 1929. This is the only Mississippi River rail crossing between Baton Rouge and Memphis and is the only highway crossing between Natchez and Greenville. In 1973, completion of Interstate 20 provided a complete four lane bridge over the river. Freight rail traffic still crosses via the old bridge, however. North and south transportation links occur on the Mississippi River and U.S. Highway 61.

Maps and information can be found at the **Vicksburg Convention and Visitors Bureau**, which is located at 52 Old Highway 27. Contact (601) 636-9421 or (800) 221-3536.

VICKSBURG NATIONAL MILITARY PARK

Vicksburg National Military Park is the site of the Battle of Vicksburg during the American Civil War which occurred in 1863 and was a crucial turning point in the war. The campaign for Vicksburg is considered by many military historians to have been the most critical campaign of the Civil War, as it severed the Confederacy geographically and cut vital supply lines to the Confederate States and thus was pivotal in the defeat of the Confederacy. Victory at Vicksburg gave Union forces control of the Mississippi River. The park commemorates the campaign, siege, and defense of Vicksburg in 1863 and includes over 1,340 monuments, markers, and plaques. The **Visitor Center** at the park offers general and historical information, a 20 minute orientation film, exhibits on various topics of the Civil War period, a bookstore, restroom facilities, and regional information. The park is located at 3201 Clay Street and admission is required. Hours: Mon.-Fri. 8-5 P.M. Contact (601) 636-0583.

The **USS Cairo Museum** at the Vicksburg National Military Park offers general and historical information, exhibits on naval operations of the Civil War, a bookstore, restroom facilities, and a picnic area. Artifacts on display are a time capsule of life aboard an ironclad gunboat. Sailors' personal possessions, cookware, medical supplies, and weaponry are featured. A six-minute video explains the sinking, discovery, and salvage operations of the gunboat. The **U.S.S. Cairo** was one of seven ironclad gunboats named in honor of towns along the upper Mississippi and Ohio rivers. These powerful ironclads were formidable vessels, each

43

mounting thirteen big guns or cannons. The museum is located at 3201 Clay Street and admission is required. Hours: Mon.-Sun. 8:30-5 P.M. Contact: (601) 636-2199.

Three detached units at the park include the riverfront batteries at **Navy Circle**, **South Fort**, and **Louisiana Circle**. Across the Mississippi River is the last remaining section of **Grant's Canal**, where Union forces attempted to bypass Vicksburg by digging a channel through DeSoto Point. Exhibits include a historic state highway marker, bronze tablet and wayside exhibits on Williams Canal, Grant's Canal, Black Troops at Milliken's Bend, and the Connecticut State Monument, dedicated in 2008.

Pemberton's Headquarters was the residence and operations center of Confederate General John Pemberton during the siege of Vicksburg. The mansion was built in 1835 by William Bobb in the Greek Revival style and is located on the bluffs of the Mississippi River. The mansion, one of the finest in Vicksburg, is located in downtown Vicksburg at 1018 Crawford Street. Contact (601) 636-0583 for operating hours.

Tour options for Vicksburg National Military Park include self-guided driving tours using the official park brochure and map. Licensed park tour guides are available and can be arranged for individuals or groups for a fee. A 16-mile **tour road** parallels Union siege and Confederate defensive lines, with three interconnecting roadways, 15 designated tour stops, wayside markers and exhibits, and short spur trails to points of interest. Keep in mind that the summers in Vicksburg are very hot and that the park is mostly outdoor except for the Visitor Center. The park itself is described as having natural beauty.

Containing 116 acres, **Vicksburg National Cemetery** is the largest burial place of Civil War casualties in the nation with nearly 17,000 Union soldiers buried here. There are at least three known Confederates buried in Vicksburg National Cemetery, two of whom have graves designated by Confederate headstones. The cemetery is located at 3201 Clay Street. Hours: Daily 8-5 P.M. Contact (601) 636-0583.

Cedar Hill Cemetery contains the graves of Vicksburg citizens spanning 150 years and includes the graves of 5,000 Confederate soldiers who died during the Siege of Vicksburg. The cemetery is located at 326 Lovers Lane. Contact: (601) 634-4513.

MUSEUMS

The **Old Depot Museum** features a 250 square foot diorama of the battlefield at Vicksburg with 2,300 miniature soldiers and the presentation of the film "The Vanishing Glory". The museum also contains 250 ship models including tow boats, riverboats, gunboats, and navy vessels. In addition, railroad models, artwork, and Civil War artifacts are on display. The museum is located at 1010 Levee Street and admission is charged. Hours: Mon.-Sat. 9-5 P.M. Contact (601) 638-6500.

Riverfront Murals have recently been painted on the floodwall on Levee Street. Local artist Robert Dafford has painted 32 pictorial murals showcasing periods in the history of Vicksburg. One mural is by Martha Ferris. The **Old Courthouse Museum** is located inside a historic structure built in 1858 and features Civil War artifacts, portraits, antique furniture, and many unique artifacts. The courthouse is the most historic building in Vicksburg. Four porticos or porches supported by 30 foot ionic columns describe the exterior of the two story building. The museum is located at 1008 Cherry Street and admission is charged. Hours: Mon.-Sat. 8:30-4:30, Sun. 1:30-4:30. Contact (601) 636-0741.

The **Lower Mississippi River Museum and Riverfront Interpretive Site** is a free museum that focuses on life on the river. Topics include the history of the Mississippi River, the science behind water movement, and future plans for the Mississippi Valley. The museum features a theater, display exhibits, a wall mural, the mission of the Corps of Engineers, and a 1,500 gallon aquarium. The museum is located at 910

Washington Street and admission is free. Hours: Tue.-Sat. 9-5 P.M. Contact (601) 638-9900.

Vicksburg is the location of the first bottled Coca-Cola®, which occurred in 1894 inside a restored 1890 building that houses the **Biedenharn Coca-Cola® Museum**. The museum contains reproduction bottling works, Coca-Cola® memorabilia, a 1900 soda fountain, and an 1890 restored candy store. The museum is located at 1107 Washington Street and admission is required. Hours: Mon.-Sat. 9-5 P.M., Sun. 1:30-4:30 P.M. Contact (601) 638-6514.

Yesterday's Children Antique Doll and Toy Museum houses one of the largest collections of rare 19th and 20th century French and German bisque dolls. The museum also includes teddy bears, trains, cars, G.I. Joe, and a variety of antique toys. The museum is located at 1104 Washington Street and admission is required. Hours: Mon.-Sat. 10-4 P.M. Contact (601) 638-0650.

SHOPPING

Shopping in Vicksburg is available at **Levee Street** in downtown and features retail shops, restaurants, museums, art galleries, and antique shops. The **Outlets at Vicksburg** offers nationally known clothing brands at discounted prices and is located at 4000 South Frontage Street. Hours: Mon.-Thu. 10-8 P.M., Fri.-Sat. 10-9 P.M., Sun. 12-6 P.M. Contact: (601) 636-7434.

DINING IN VICKSBURG

Rusty's Riverfront Grill is located at 901 Washington Street and serves a variety of steaks, seafood, and pasta. Contact (601) 638-2030. Hours: Tue.-Fri. 11 A.M.-2 P.M., 5-9:30 P.M., Sat. 11 A.M.-9:30 P.M.

Roca Restaurant serves European-influenced cuisine with a southern flavor in an upscale setting and is located at 127 Country Club Drive. Contact (601) 638-0800. Hours: Tue.-Thu. 11-2 P.M. and 5-9 P.M., Fri. 11-2 P.M. and 5-10 P.M., Sat. 5-10 P.M., Sun. 11-2 P.M.

FESTIVALS AND EVENTS

Tapestry: The Pilgrimage to Vicksburg is an event that showcases the historic homes and buildings in the city and the history associated with them. The history and culture of the antebellum age and the Siege of Vicksburg are part of the history in which these buildings are associated. The event is held throughout the month of April. Contact (800) 221-3536.

The **Riverfest Music and Arts Festival** features live music concerts and performers in a variety of music genres along with arts and crafts. Vicksburg's premier music and arts festival, Riverfest is an annual event and has been a tradition since 1987. The event is held in late April. Contact (601) 634-4527.

The **Vicksburg Fall Fest** features live music, sidewalk sales, a bike ride, children's activities, and a flea market in downtown. The annual Fall Fest has been held since 1994 in October. Contact (601) 634-4527.

NATCHEZ

Jackson-Evers International Airport is located 130 miles northeast of Natchez. Highway 61 and the Natchez Trace Parkway provide access to Natchez from Vicksburg and Jackson.

HISTORY

Natchez is located on the Mississippi River in southwest Mississippi. Founded in 1716 by the French, Natchez is one of the oldest settlements in the lower Mississippi River Valley region. The city was originally known as Fort Rosalie but was later named after the Native American tribe who inhabited the area. Natchez served as the capital of the Mississippi Territory from its creation in 1798 although the state legislature sometimes gathered in nearby Washington, Mississippi. The Capital was permanently moved to Jackson in 1822.

Natchez became a center of trade and commerce with the Native American, European, and African-American cultures in the region from the early 1700's to late 1800's. Many large **antebellum style homes** or "pre-Civil War mansions" were built in the 1800's by wealthy southern planters who sold their crops through the Natchez port. These homes are the central tourist attraction in the area. Natchez is also home to many **African-American historical sites**, including churches, neighborhoods, and homes. After 1900, Natchez experienced an economic downturn from the replacement of river traffic with railroads and the loss of industry. However, tourism in the city has remained strong. Natchez has over 500 antebellum or pre-Civil War structures still remaining.

The **Natchez Visitor Center** is located at 640 South Canal Street. Contact: (601) 446-6345.

HISTORIC HOMES

The **Natchez Pilgrimage Tours** features more than 25 antebellum mansion tours which are given during a five-week period every spring and fall. Several of these mansions are **National Historic Landmarks** including Longwood, Magnolia Hall, Melrose, Monmouth Plantation, Rosalie and Stanton Hall. The tours offer musical productions, theatre, and historical presentations. The tours office is located at 640 South Canal Street. Contact (601) 446-6631 or (800) 647-6742. **Carriage**

rides are also available at the Canal Street Depot daily 9-4 P.M., weather permitting. Night tours are also available. Contact (601) 442-4581.

Longwood is an antebellum mansion in Natchez and is the largest octagonal shaped home in North America. Built by Dr. Haller Nutt for his wife and family, the Oriental Revival style home has six floors and an onion-shaped dome top with a pointed spire. Architect Samuel Sloan of Philadelphia designed the home in 1859. While most of the exterior of the home was competed, the interior of the home was left unfinished as the Civil War began and the craftsmen went home. Nutt died of pneumonia in 1864 and the mansion was never completed. The first floor of the interior was completed and the Nutt family lived there while the upper floors were left unfinished. Longwood is one of the most photographed mansions in Natchez and is a must see for visitors. Longwood is located at 140 Lower Woodville Road. Hours: 9-4:30 daily. Contact (601) 442-5193.

Magnolia Hall was the last large mansion built in Natchez before the Civil War. This Greek Revival style mansion was built in 1858 by merchant Thomas Henderson and was later owned by the Britton family. The mansion features a Henderson family museum collection of pilgrimage costumes and a doll collection. The Natchez Garden Club has restored the mansion. Magnolia Hall is located at 215 South Pearl Street. Hours: Fri.-Sun. 10-5 P.M. Contact (601) 442-6672 or (800) 647-6742.

Melrose is a two story Greek Revival mansion built in 1848. The site also contains slave quarters, a landscaped park, and formal gardens. Melrose is part of Natchez National Historic Park, which is located at One Melrose Montebello Parkway. The mansion represents the height of Southern prosperity and the "Cotton Kingdom." Melrose was built by the John T. McMurran family beginning in 1841. McMurran's daughter-in-law Alice Austen described the mansion as "very elegant" and "one of the handsomest places I have seen north or south." Guided tours of the home give visitors a glimpse into the lifestyle of the pre-Civil War American South and help them understand the roles that slaves played in an estate setting. Sitting today on 80 lush acres and maintained by the National Park Service, the home stands as a well-preserved piece of America's history. Melrose is located at One Melrose-Montebello Parkway. Hours: 9-4 P.M. daily. Contact (601) 446-5790.

The **William Johnson House** is also part of Natchez National Historic Park. The house consists of the original Johnson home and the adjoining McCallum House. William Johnson, a free black barber in Natchez, used bricks from buildings destroyed in the infamous tornado of 1840 to construct the State Street estate and commercial business area. The family lived in the upper stories of the house, while the first floor was rented out to merchants. The William Johnson House, renovated by the National Park Service, allows visitors to learn more about the life of free African Americans in the pre-Civil War South. Visitors to the home will also learn about the extensive diary kept by William Johnson from 1835-1851, which detailed everyday life in Natchez. The William Johnson House is located at 210 State Street. Hours: 9-4:30 P.M. daily. Contact (601) 445-5345.

Rosalie is a Federal style mansion and was named for the nearby French fort, which later became known as Natchez. This three story mansion is a National Historic Landmark and was built by Peter Little in 1823 on the Natchez bluffs. Peter Little and his wife Eliza lived in the home until Eliza passed in 1853 and Peter passed in 1856. Rosalie served as Union headquarters during the Civil War. After several ownership changes, the mansion was sold to the Mississippi State Society, Daughters of the American Revolution in 1938. Rosalie also features landscaped gardens surrounding the mansion. Rosalie Mansion is located at 100 Orleans Street and admission is required for entrance. Hours: 9-4 P.M. daily. Contact (601) 445-4555.

Stanton Hall was built in 1858 by cotton broker Frederick Stanton for his family in the Classical Revival style. The mansion and property covers an entire city block and is surrounded by live oak trees. Stanton Hall has ceilings over 16 feet tall and a 70 foot hallway. Carriage House Restaurant is located adjacent to Stanton Hall and is a popular dining establishment in Natchez. Stanton Hall is a National Historic Landmark and is located at 401 High Street. Hours: 9-4 P.M. daily. Contact (601) 442-6282 or (800) 647-6742.

Auburn was the first antebellum home in Natchez to follow an architectural plan. This Greek Revival style mansion has a unique feature- an unsupported spiral staircase leading to the second floor. Lyman Harding employed Levi Weeks to design and build Auburn Mansion in 1811. In the 1830's, two symmetrical wings were added to the mansion by Dr. Stephen Duncan. The Auburn Mansion is a National Historic Landmark and is located at 400 Duncan Avenue. Hours: Tue.-Sat. 11-3 P.M. Contact (601) 442-5981.

The **House on Ellicot Hill** is a Federal Style home built between 1798 and 1801, which was before most of the large mansions in Natchez. The two-story home is one of the oldest homes in Natchez and is the site of a historical event. In 1797, Andrew Ellicot was commissioned by President Washington to survey the area after the United States had acquired the area from Spain. Ellicot raised the flag of the United States on this hill, the hill in which the house is built. The house is a National Historic Landmark and is located at 211 North Canal Street. Hours: Fri.-Sat. 10-3 P.M. Contact (601) 442-2011.

Linden is a two story Federal style home built in the late 1700's and has operated as a bed and breakfast for several decades. The home is located in a seven acre park-like setting. Linden has been owned by the same family for six generations. The east wing was added to the home in 1818. The home is located at 1 Linden Place. Contact: (601) 445-5472 or (800) 254-6336.

The **Towers** is a two story mansion built in 1796 and features an Italianate exterior which was added before the Civil War. Two third-story towers were originally part of the mansion, however one was destroyed by fire and the other was removed. The mansion contains an extensive collection of antique period furniture along with two luxury suites for guests. Five acres of gardens surround the mansion. The Towers is located at 801 Myrtle Avenue. Contact: (601) 446-6890.

HISTORIC HOTELS

Monmouth Mansion was the home of General John A. Quitman, an early Mississippi Governor. Built in 1818, the mansion is also surrounded by formal gardens and operates as a luxury hotel and restaurant. The mansion is also a National Historic Landmark. The mansion is located at 36 Melrose Avenue. Hours: 10 A.M. daily. Tours are available during pilgrimages. Contact (601) 442-5852 or (800) 828-4531.

Dunleith is a Greek Revival style mansion built by Charles Dahlgren and also operates as a historic hotel. The mansion was built in 1856 when the original mansion on the site was struck by lightning and burned to the ground. The 40 acre estate includes a 1790's carriage house, greenhouse, and a three story brick building. The Dunleith Mansion has 26 Tuscan columns and porches on the first and second floors. Dunleith is located at 84 Homochitto Street. Contact (601) 446-8500 or (800) 433-2445.

HISTORIC SITES

Natchez National Cemetery is the burial place of 3,000 Union soldiers from the Civil War and famous citizens of historic Natchez. Natchez National Cemetery dates to 1866, one of 21 national cemeteries established in that year. Located on a bluff overlooking the Mississippi River, the site's topography influenced its unique layout of irregular shaped burial sections, terraced hillsides, and gravel and grass pathways. The cemetery is located at 41 Cemetery Road and is open daily dawn to dusk. Contact (601) 445-4981.

The **Natchez Museum of African-American History and Culture** contains exhibits and information focusing on the history and heritage of African-Americans in Natchez and the surrounding area. African Americans had an important part in the history of Natchez including many stories that many have not heard and this museum helps tell those stories. The museum is located at 301 Main Street and admission is required. Hours: Tue.-Sat. 1-4:30 P.M. Contact (601) 445-0728.

Historic Jefferson College opened its doors on January 7, 1811 as a preparatory school with fifteen students. Funds from Congress, the Legislature, and private citizens led the way to new prosperity, and by 1817 Jefferson College had become completely operational. As the most impressive educational institution of the Natchez region, Jefferson College quickly became a center of the intellectual community. The outbreak of the Civil War forced the closing of Jefferson College in 1863 but the college reopened in 1866. Jefferson College remained a preparatory school and by the beginning of the twentieth century, the school had become known as Jefferson Military College. The college closed permanently in 1964 because of declining enrollment. Historic Jefferson College is located at Highway 61 North in Washington, Mississippi. Hours: Mon.-Sat. 9-5 P.M., Sun. 1-5 P.M. Contact (601) 442-2901.

Natchez Trace Parkway was the first route to enter Natchez and was originally a buffalo trail. The parkway path was later used by Native Americans and European settlers. In the early 1800's boatmen from the Ohio River Valley floated cash crops, livestock, and other materials down the Mississippi River on wooden flatboats. At Natchez or New Orleans, they sold their goods, sold their boats for lumber, and walked or rode horseback toward home on the Old Trace. The Natchez Trace became obsolete after the arrival of the steamboat and is now administered by the National Park Service. Today, the Natchez Trace includes a two lane highway that runs 450 miles between Natchez and Nashville, Tennessee. No commercial development is allowed on the parkway including billboards and this allows the parkway to have a scenic feel. Some of the old paths on the Trace (the Sunken Trace) have been preserved and are available for hiking at milepost 41.5. The paved portion of the Trace is popular with bicyclists in addition to motorists. Contact (800) 305-7417.

Loess Bluffs can be seen from the Natchez Trace Parkway at milepost 12.4. Loess is a wind-blown sediment deposit believed to have been transported from glacial lands. Loess is found in certain parts of the world and commonly forms steep vertical cliffs or bluffs.

Natchez Under-the-Hill is the location of the historic flatboat and steamboat landing on the Mississippi River. This historic district is bounded by South Canal Street, Broadway Street, and the Mississippi River. This district once contained the whole city, which included about 20 buildings in the 1770's. The district was popular because it was the last stop for boatmen on the Mississippi River before New Orleans. In the 1800's, taverns, gambling halls and brothels were located in the district and knife fights and killings were common. Slaves were also sold in this district. Eventually the Natchez slave owners tried to get rid of the district by taxing the boats and eventually expelled the boatmen. The district lost much traffic when railroads were completed in the late 19th Century and in 1940 when the Mississippi River Bridge was constructed the district became a ghost town. In the 1970's more traffic appeared when travel tour boats began operation. Today several restaurants are located in the district.

HISTORIC CHURCHES

St. Mary Basilica was built in 1842 and is the oldest Catholic Church in Mississippi. Considered an architectural masterpiece among Catholic churches in the South, the Neo-Gothic style church remains in operation today. Completion of the church took 44 years until 1886 but mass has been held in the church since 1843 while construction continued. The church is located at 107 South Union Street. Hours: 7 A.M. to sunset. Contact (601) 445-5616.

Temple B'nai Israel was built in 1905 for the Jewish community in the area and continues to attract a few members. The Jewish community in Natchez was once larger, however. B'nai Israel began in 1843 and is the oldest functioning Jewish congregation in Mississippi. The temple features tall ceilings, an exterior dome, and stained glass windows. The temple can be found at 213 South Commerce Street. Contact (601) 445-5407.

Trinity Episcopal Church is the oldest church building in Natchez and the oldest Episcopal Church in Mississippi. Built in 1822, the church was renovated to the Greek Revival style. The first service was held in 1823 and the services continue today. The church is located at 305 South Commerce Street. Hours: Mon.-Fri. 9-4 P.M. Contact (601) 445-8432.

NATIVE AMERICAN SITES

Emerald Mound is one of the largest Native American mounds in North America and is a designated National Historic Landmark. Covering eight acres, Emerald Mound measures 770 feet by 435 feet at the base and is 35 feet high. The mound was built by depositing earth soil along the sides of a natural hill, thus reshaping it and creating an enormous artificial plateau. Two smaller mounds sit on top of the expansive summit platform of the primary mound. The larger of the two, at the west end, measures 190 feet by 160 feet and is 30 feet high. Several additional smaller mounds were once located along the edges of the primary mound summit, but were destroyed in the 19th century by plowing and erosion. Emerald Mound, built and used during the Mississippian period between 1250 and 1600 A.D., was a ceremonial center for the local population, which resided in outlying villages and hamlets. The Emerald Mound builders were ancestors of the Natchez Indians. By the late 1600s, the Natchez had abandoned Emerald Mound and established their capital at the Grand Village some 12 miles to the southwest. Emerald Mound is located at the Natchez Trace Parkway at the 10.3 milepost (about 10 miles northeast of Natchez). Hours: Daily, dawn to dusk. Contact (601) 445-4211 or (800) 305-7417.

The **Grand Village of the Natchez Indians** is a National Historic Landmark and the ceremonial mound center for the Natchez Indians. Three platform mounds, an adjacent ceremonial plaza and associated habitation areas mark the political and religious capital of the Natchez Indian chiefdom of the late 17th century and early 18th century. A number of French colonists who witnessed the use of the mounds at Grand Village recorded their observations. The paramount chief of the Natchez, called the Great Sun, lived at the Grand Village. Elaborate funeral ceremonies for the Natchez elite were conducted on the mound plaza. Continued French settlement in the area led to a Natchez invasion of the French Fort Rosalie in which most of the French there were killed. The French soon retaliated and attacked the Natchez with help from the Choctaw Indians. Most of the Natchez tribe left the area after the attack. A museum is on the site and admission is free. The Grand Village is located at 400 Jefferson Davis Boulevard. Hours: Mon.-Sat. 9-5 P.M. Sun. 1:30-5 P.M. Contact (601) 446-6502.

DINING IN NATCHEZ

Magnolia Grill is located at 49 Silver Street. Contact (601) 446-7670. Hours: Tue.-Thu. 11-9 P.M., Fri.-Sat. 11-10 P.M., Sun. 11-9 P.M.

Slick Rick's Foods (organic and gourmet) is located at 109 North Pearl Street. Contact (601) 445-9900. Hours: Mon.-Thu. 10 A.M.-4 P.M., Fri.-Sat. 10 A.M.-6 P.M.

FESTIVALS AND EVENTS

The **Natchez Spring Pilgrimage** is a four week event that has been held since 1932 and features 29 antebellum mansions on tour. Visitors can learn about the antebellum age during the tour from guides wearing costumes from the time period. Many of the guides are descendants of the original home owners. The pilgrimage is held during the months of March and April. A second pilgrimage event or **Fall Pilgrimage** is held for three weeks in late September and early October. Contact (800) 647-6742.

The **Natchez Festival of Music** features a variety of world-class music and theater including opera, Broadway, and jazz. Nationally and internationally known performers are also sponsored by the four week festival, which has been a tradition since 1990 and is held the entire month of May. Contact (601) 445-2210.

The **Natchez Powwow** celebration features the Native American heritage of Natchez and has been held annually since 1988. The annual event is held in March and features traditional Native American dancing and singing, traditional foods, crafted jewelry and art at the Grand Village of the Natchez Indians. Contact (601) 442-0200.

The **Natchez Food and Wine Festival** features the works of some of the best chefs in the South and draws visitors from neighboring states and the region. The festival has been a tradition since 2000 and is held in late July. Contact (800) 647-6724.

PORT GIBSON

Port Gibson is one of the oldest cities in Mississippi and is located about 47 miles northeast of Natchez by way of Highway 61 or the Natchez Trace Parkway. Port Gibson is an important stop on the route between Natchez, Vicksburg, and Jackson because of its historical attractions. Port Gibson was founded in 1802 by Samuel Gibson and is the county seat of Claiborne County. Port Gibson is known as the city "too beautiful to burn", as proclaimed by U.S. Major General Ulysses S. Grant during the Civil War, according to local legend. Port Gibson is a small town with around 2,000 residents, however the several historical attractions located here are worth the stop.

The **Port Gibson Chamber of Commerce** provides information and maps and is located at 1601 Church Street. Contact (601) 437-4351.

WINDSOR RUINS

Windsor, built between 1859 and 1861, was the home of Smith Coffee Daniel, II, a wealthy planter who had extensive properties in the Delta and in Arkansas. Designed by David Shroder and completed in 1861, the home was the largest antebellum mansion in Mississippi and the plantation once covered over 2,600 acres. From the elaborate furnishings to the wrought iron staircase, the four-story home was designed to reflect the height of southern life at the time. The mansion contained 25 rooms and 25 fireplaces. The home survived the Civil War only to be totally destroyed on February 17, 1890 by a fire said to have been caused by a party guest who carelessly dropped a cigarette.

Today the remains of Windsor include 23 Corinthian columns on the site. The family descendants of the Windsor owners donated the property to the State Department of Archives in 1974 and the Archives continues to maintain the site today. The wrought iron staircase is now a part of nearby Alcorn State University. Windsor Ruins has appeared in several feature films, including *Raintree County* (1957), which starred Elizabeth Taylor and Montgomery Cliff.

Windsor Ruins is located 12 miles southwest of Port Gibson on Mississippi Highway 552 (or 15095 Rodney Road). Contact (601) 437-4351.

CIVIL WAR SITES

The **Grand Gulf Military Park** is dedicated to preserving the memory of both the town and the battle which occurred in the town of Grand Gulf. This 400 acre landmark is listed on the National Register of Historic Places. The park includes Fort Cobun and Fort Wade, the Grand Gulf Cemetery, a museum, campgrounds, picnic areas, hiking trails, an observation tower, and several restored buildings dating back to the heyday of Grand Gulf. At the museum visitors can trace the development of Grand Gulf through early photographs, maps, scale models, and authentic artifacts found in the area. Coaches and carriages could be found in Grand Gulf when it was bustling with people. Union and Confederate uniforms, cannon balls, and muskets remain from the fighting that took place during the latter stage of the Civil War. The park is located eight miles northwest of Port Gibson at 12006 Grand Gulf Road and admission is required. Contact (601) 437-5911. Hours: daily 8-5 P.M.

The town of Grand Gulf began in the early 1800's as a port village and was incorporated in 1835. By the late 1850's Grand Gulf was an important port and trading center with 1,000 residents and 76 city blocks. Yellow fever, a tornado, and the changing course of the Mississippi River reduced the population greatly. Civil War battles completely destroyed the town except for a few antebellum buildings. Today, Grand Gulf is a ghost town.

The **Port Gibson Battlefield** is the site of the battle in which Union forces led by General Ulysses S. Grant were victorious over the Confederate forces. The battle was part of the Vicksburg Campaign in which Union forces eventually captured the city of Vicksburg. Grant's forces travelled up Rodney Road (which still exists today) toward Port Gibson. The battlefield is located at Old Rodney Road at Point Lookout. Contact (601) 446-6502 for hours and information. Civil War soldiers, generals, and residents including the Samuel Gibson family are buried at historic **Wintergreen Cemetery**, which is located at 613 Greenwood Street. Hours: 8-5 P.M. daily. Contact (601) 437-8846.

HISTORIC DISTRICT

The Port Gibson historic district includes **City Hall**, an 1840 Greek Revival style building which also displays historic photographs of the city. City Hall is located at 1005 College Street. Contact (601) 437-4234 for hours. The historic district also includes the **Engelson House**, the site of the oldest formal gardens in Mississippi. Contact (601) 437-4351. The **Claiborne County Courthouse** has an impressive architectural style including a dome top at 410 Market Street. Contact (601) 437-4351.

First Presbyterian Church is located at 605 Church Street and features a sculpted golden hand on the steeple "pointing toward heaven." Contact (601) 437-4351. **Saint Joseph Catholic Church** is the oldest church in Port Gibson, constructed in 1849 in the Gothic Revival style and is located at 909 Church Street. Hours: Mon.-Fri. 9-3 P.M. Contact (601) 437-4351.

Temple Gemiluth Chessed is a Moorish Revival style synagogue which is the oldest surviving synagogue in Mississippi and the only building of this architectural style. Built in 1892 by Jewish immigrants of German ancestry, the congregation closed in 1986 because of declining population. The temple is located at 708 Church Street. Contact (601) 437-4708.

DINING IN PORT GIBSON

Best Wok is located at 1091 Highway 61. Hours: Mon.-Thu. 11-10 P.M., Fri.-Sat. 11-11 P.M., Sun. 12-10 P.M. Contact (601) 437-0079.

RODNEY

The ghost town of Rodney is located on Rodney Road southwest of Port Gibson and just west of the Alcorn State University campus. Rodney was originally a French settlement in 1763 and was named Petit Gouffre. Great Britain and Spain later controlled the area until it became part of the United States in the early 1800's. Rodney once had several hundred residents and was three votes away from being named the capital of the Mississippi Territory. Rodney boasted several churches and a grocery store. The population declined because the Mississippi River shifted course.

The **Rodney Center Historic District** is listed on the National Register of Historical Places. A small number of people live in the area but Rodney is considered a ghost town and is not recognized by the U.S. Census Bureau. During General Ulysses Grant's campaign to capture Vicksburg, Rodney was heavily shelled by Union Naval forces. A cannonball is embedded into the exterior wall of **Rodney Presbyterian Church**, which can be seen today. The Alston Grocery Store building and a two story brick building also remain standing today, along with

61

residential homes and the 1850 Baptist Church. Contact (601) 853-0230 for more information.

CHURCH HILL

Church Hill is a small unincorporated town about 18 miles north of Natchez with settlers originally from Maryland in the late 1700's. The town is located on the steep bluffs of the Mississippi River and was once a thriving town. At the center of this small town is an old wooden country store and post office with the name "**Wagner's Grocery**" on the front of the building. The store, one of the oldest known such structures in the southeastern Unites States, was built around 1837 and was in operation until the late 1990's. Also in the town center is **Christ Church**, a structure that was completed in 1858 in the style of a Gothic Revival English country church. The church congregation was originally organized in the 1790's.

Several privately owned antebellum homes also exist in the Church Hill community but are not open to the public. Several prominent families lived here including Thomas Marston Green, a wealthy planter who later served in Congress. His mansion in Church Hill was the site of **Andrew Jackson's** marriage to Rachel Robards in 1791. Church Hill is located at Highway 553 and Church Hill Road. Bicycling is popular on this route of Highway 553, which loops around the Natchez Trace Parkway. Contact (601) 786-3982 for more information about the historic Church Hill community.

UNION CHURCH

The historical small town of **Union Church** is located in eastern Jefferson County and about 40 miles east of Natchez. The earliest European settlers were of Scottish origin and came to Union Church in the early 1800's from North Carolina. Several historic churches exist in Union Church. **Union Church Presbyterian Church** is the third oldest Presbyterian Church in Mississippi and was organized in 1817. The existing Presbyterian church building was built in 1852. There were also a few Methodist worshipers in Union Church who lacked the resources to start their own church and worshiped with the Presbyterians. Union Commander **Benjamin Grierson** and his cavalry raid crossed through Union Church in 1863 during the Civil War and the Vicksburg Campaign. Union Church is located 40 miles east of Natchez on Highway 28. Contact (601) 786-3982 for more information about the historic Union Church community.

LORMAN

The small unincorporated community of **Lorman** is located in Jefferson County, about 9 miles north of Fayette and 32 miles northeast of Natchez on Highway 61. Lorman is known as the home of Alcorn State University. **Rosswood Plantation** was located on a 1,250 acre cotton plantation (now 100 acres) and features a Greek Revival style mansion originally owned by Dr. Walter Ross Wade. Originally built in 1857, the completely restored mansion has 14 rooms with 14 foot ceilings, 10 fireplaces, a winding stairway, antiques, and furnishings from around the world. The mansion was designed by David Shroder, the architect of Windsor nearby. The plantation also operates as a bed and breakfast and is located at 2513 Red Lick Road by way of Highway 552 east of

Lorman. The plantation is open March to November only. Contact (601) 437-4215 or (800) 533-5889.

The **Old Country Store Restaurant** is located on Highway 61 in Lorman and is known for its southern food. The restaurant offers a buffet featuring fried chicken, ribs, vegetables, and deserts. Owned by Arthur Davis, the restaurant has been featured on the Food Network. The restaurant is located at 18801 Highway 61 South. Contact (601) 437-3661.

WOODVILLE

Woodville is one of the oldest towns in Mississippi and was incorporated in 1811. Woodville is located in the southwest corner of Mississippi and is the county seat of Wilkinson County. Woodville is home to the oldest operating newspaper in Mississippi, the **Woodville Republican**, founded in 1823. The timber industry is important to the economy of Woodville.

The Woodville historic district includes more than 100 buildings including a courthouse square. The oldest existing bank building in Mississippi is included in the historic district and now houses the **African American Museum**. At the museum visitors can learn about William Grant Still, who was born in Woodville. Still became the first African-American to conduct a major orchestra when he conducted the Los Angeles Symphony in 1936. Contact (601) 888-7151.

Also in the historic district is the 1824 **St. Paul Episcopal Church**, which was one of the founding parishes of the Episcopal Church in Mississippi and is located on Church Street. Contact (601) 888-3177 for hours.

Just south of Woodville on Highway 61 is the **Mississippi Welcome Center**, where visitors can receive tourism information about the area and the state of Mississippi. The **Wilkinson County Museum** can provide information about local historic sites and other tourist information. The museum is located at the courthouse square and Bank Street. Contact (601) 888-7151.

Rosemont Plantation was the childhood home of Jefferson Davis and his family. Jefferson Davis was the President of the Confederate States of America from 1861 to 1865. This Federal style home was built by the parents of Jefferson Davis in 1810 and contains mostly original furnishings. The Davis family lived in the home until 1895. The home is located at 921 Highway 24 East and admission is required. Hours: Tue.-Sat. 10-4:30 P.M. Contact (601) 888-6809.

Clark Creek Natural Area is one of the most beautiful places in the state of Mississippi. Known for its waterfalls, Clark Creek contains over 700 acres and at least 50 waterfalls have been identified ranging in height from 10 to 30 feet. Not all waterfalls are located on established trails, however. Clark Creek has steep loess hills, hardwood and pine forest including beech and magnolia trees, a variety of birds, invertebrates, poisonous snakes, and several endangered species. Black bear have also been spotted in Clark Creek. Bird watching, hiking, and photography are popular on the established trails. Hunting, camping, and vehicles are not allowed at Clark Creek. No water or other amenities are available at Clark Creek so visitors should bring water, along with food and first aid supplies. There are two trails: a less difficult main trail and a more difficult "primitive" trail, which is known to be very strenuous. This hike is for the physically fit so older individuals and small children should not attempt the hike.

Crowds at Clark Creek are common on the weekend. Clark Creek is located west of Woodville by way of Highway 24 near the town of **Fort Adams**. Visitors can also travel west of Woodville on Pinckneyville Road to Clark Creek. Contact (601) 888-6040. Near Clark Creek is an old country store which overlooks a pond. The **"Pond Store"** is open most weekends or by appointment and is located at 182 Fort Adams-Pond Road. Hours: Fri.-Sat. 8-5 P.M., Sun. 1-5 P.M. Contact (601) 888-4426.

DINING IN WOODVILLE

M&M Hot Tamales is located at 138 Prentiss Highway. Contact (601) 888-3738.

BROOKHAVEN

Brookhaven is located in southwest Mississippi 56 miles south of Jackson and at the intersection of Interstate 55 and Highway 84. Brookhaven is the county seat of Lincoln County, which was created in 1870 and was named after President Abraham Lincoln. Brookhaven was named after Brookhaven, New York, the home of Samuel Jayne, who was an early settler. The **Brookhaven-Lincoln Chamber of Commerce** is located at 230 Whitworth Avenue. Contact (601) 833-1411 or (800) 613-4667. A historic district containing one of Mississippi's largest collections of Victorian mansions and homes is located on South Jackson Street.

Historic Whitworth College was founded in Brookhaven in 1858 and was named for Rev. Milton J. Whitworth, who donated the land and the buildings for the college. The Methodist College was used as a hospital during the Civil War and was eventually closed in the 1930's. The **Mississippi School of the Arts** was established at the historic Whitworth College in 1999 and a renovation and construction process began to prepare the campus for artistically talented high school students. The school is located at 110 South Jackson Street. Contact (601) 823-1300.

The **Ole Brook Festival** is Mississippi's Premier Family Festival and is held in historic downtown Brookhaven in October. The festival features live music, entertainment for all ages, over 200 booths with food, arts and crafts, a 5K run, and a classic car show. The festival has been a tradition since 1974. Contact (601) 833-1411.

MCCOMB

Chartered in 1872, the city of **McComb** is located in South Mississippi near the intersection of Interstate 55 and Highway 98. McComb was founded by railroad company executive Colonel H.S. McComb, who purchased land and moved his railroad company to the present site of the city. Today, McComb is a regional business and healthcare center and is the largest city in Pike County.

Percy Quin State Park is a nice stop just off Interstate 55 near McComb and the Louisiana border. The park was constructed in the 1930's and features campgrounds and cabins, golf, fishing, boating, water skiing, camp store, tennis, and hiking trails. Admission is required. The park is located on Percy Quin Drive and can be found by taking Exit 13 from Interstate 55, Airport Fernwood Road, and Highway 48 North. Contact (601) 684-3938. For dining options near McComb, try **Dinner Bell Restaurant** for Southern cooking at 229 5th Avenue. Contact (601) 684-4883. Hours: Tue.-Sun. 11-2 P.M.

SOUTHEAST MISSISSIPPI REGION

Southeast Mississippi contains the towns of Hattiesburg, Laurel, Collins, and Columbia. Interstate 59 runs northeast-southwest and connects Laurel and Hattiesburg to Meridian and Picayune. Highway 49 runs northwest-southeast and connects Hattiesburg to Jackson and Gulfport. Highway 84 runs east-west and connects Laurel to Collins and Brookhaven. Highway 98 also runs east-west and connects Hattiesburg to Mobile, Columbia, and McComb.

LAUREL

Laurel is a charming town in southeastern Mississippi with oak lined streets and historic homes. Established in 1892, Laurel flourished with the growth of the timber industry in the early 1900's. A railroad and a large lumber mill opened in 1893 and Laurel soon had the largest yellow pine industry in the world. The discovery of oil in 1942 and other industries also strengthened the economy of Laurel. The **Laurel Chamber of Commerce** is located at 153 Base Drive and can provide tourist information and maps. Contact: (601) 649-3031 or (800) 392-9629.

The **Lauren Rodgers Museum of Art** is the oldest art museum in Mississippi and is centered around the city's historic district and oak trees. The museum opened in 1923 and features over 2,000 items including excellent collections of European and American art, Native American baskets, British silver, and Japanese woodblock prints. Changing exhibitions are also displayed inside the museum, which also has a store and a library. The Lauren Rodgers Museum of Art can be found at 565 North Fifth Avenue in Laurel and admission is free. Hours: Tue.-Sat. 10-4:45 P.M. Sun. 1-4 P.M. Contact (601) 649-6374.

FESTIVALS AND EVENTS

The Lauren Rodgers Museum of Art in Laurel sponsors the annual **Blues Bash** in early June. The event has been a tradition since 1993 and features live blues entertainment and barbeque on the front lawn of the museum. The museum is located at 5th Avenue and Seventh Street in historic downtown Laurel. Contact (601) 649-6374.

The **South Mississippi Fair** in Laurel is one of the largest fairs in Mississippi. The fair features several dozen amusement rides for all ages, a variety of food and entertainment events for all ages, and multiple live music performances of different genres. The week-long event is held in late October at the Magnolia Center at 1457 Ellisville Boulevard. Contact (601) 649-9010.

DINING IN LAUREL

For dining options in Laurel, try **Café la Fleur**, a New Orleans style restaurant located in downtown Laurel at 313 North Magnolia Street. Hours: Mon.-Fri. 11-2 P.M., Fri. 6-9 P.M. Contact (601) 426-2100.

HATTIESBURG

Hattiesburg was founded by lawyer and railroad builder William Harris Hardy and named after his wife Hattie. Incorporated in 1884, Hattiesburg was originally a lumber and railroad industry town. Today, industry in Hattiesburg has diversified and two universities are located here along with a National Guard base. The University of Southern Mississippi, William Carey University, and Camp Shelby are major factors in the economy of Hattiesburg. Today Hattiesburg is the fourth largest city in Mississippi at around 49,000 residents. Hattiesburg is located about 70 miles north of Gulfport from Highway 49 and 88 miles southeast of Jackson from Highway 49.

The **Hattiesburg Visitor Center** can provide tourist information and maps and is located at Five Convention Center Plaza. Contact (601) 296-7475 or (866) 442-8843.

HATTIESBURG ATTRACTIONS

Historic downtown Hattiesburg is filled with shops, restaurants, and galleries. The historic **Saenger Theater** is also downtown. Built in 1929 and designed by New Orleans architect Emile Weile, the 997 seat theater originally showed silent movies. In 2000 a major renovation of the theater was completed which restored its original appearance and the theater is now listed on the National Register of Historic Places. The Saenger Theater features original lighting, lobby chandeliers, theater seating, a balcony, a stage, and the original theater pipe organ. The Saenger Theater is located at 201 Forrest Street. Contact (601) 584-4888 for schedules.

The **Mississippi Armed Forces Museum** is a free museum open to the public and is located at Camp Shelby. The museum serves as the military history museum for the state of Mississippi and features exhibits, tours, rare artifacts and memorabilia from the Civil War, two World Wars, Korea, Vietnam, and the Persian Gulf Wars. Thousands of items from all branches of the military are featured. The museum is located 12 miles south of Hattiesburg on Highway 49. Hours: Tue.-Sat. 9-4:30 P.M. Contact (601) 558-2757.

The **African American Military History Museum** was opened in 1942 and features exhibits, photographs, and artifacts focused on the military history of African Americans in all wars fought by the United States. The museum is located at 305 East Sixth Street. Hours: Tue.-Sat. 10-4 P.M. Contact (601) 450-1942.

The **Hattiesburg Zoo** is one of the most popular attractions in town. Located on 12 acres within Kamper Park, the zoo features more than 80 species of exotic animals including tigers, zebras, monkeys, iguanas, and jaguars. The zoo also features a train, carousel, splash pad, and a petting zoo. The zoo is located at Hardy Street and 17th Avenue. Hours: 10-4 P.M. Contact (601) 545-4576. **Paul Johnson State Park** offers over 800 acres of campgrounds, cabins, fishing, boating, water skiing, and nature trails. The park is located on Highway 49 about 10 miles south of Hattiesburg and is open daily. Contact (601) 582-7721.

The **All-American Rose Garden** at the University of Southern Mississippi opened in 1974 and is one of the most recognized landmarks in Hattiesburg and the region. The garden features about 800 separate bushes including hybrid tea and grandiflora professionally landscaped in alternating rows with grass. The rose bushes are in full bloom in late spring and throughout the summer. The garden is located near the intersection of Hardy Road and Highway 49. Contact (601) 266-4491.

The **Sarah Gillespie Museum of Art** is the most comprehensive collection of Mississippi art from the 20th century. Named for Hattiesburg native Sarah Gillespie, over 600 works are included in the collection using a variety of styles of drawing and painting methods. Sarah Gillespie began donating works to William Carey University in 1982 and continued during her lifetime. The gallery includes the works of Walter Anderson, Bill Dunlap, Kate Freeman Clark, John McCrady, Theora Hamblett, and Alan Flattman. The gallery can be found at 498 Tuscan Avenue at William Carey University and admission is free. Hours: Mon.-Fri. 1-4 P.M. Contact (601) 318-6107.

The **Lucille Parker Gallery** at William Carey University was named after Lucille Parker, a Mississippi native artist known for her drawings and paintings. Lucille Parker studied art at the University of Southern Mississippi, the University of Alabama, and the Pietro Venucci Academy of Art in Perugia, Italy. Parker's works are displayed across the United States. Lucille Parker also founded the art department at William Carey and was awarded an honorary doctorate from the university in 1981. The gallery also features the paintings of Mississippi artist Marie Hull and other artists from the state. The gallery is located at 512 Tuscan Avenue in Hattiesburg. Hours: Mon.-Fri. 1-4 P.M. Contact (601) 318-6192.

DINING IN HATTIESBURG

Crescent City Grill offers seafood, pasta, soups, and salads and is located at 3810 Hardy Street. Hours: Sun.-Thu. 11-10 P.M., Fri.-Sat. 11-11 P.M. Contact (601) 264-0657.

The **Purple Parrot Café** offers unique American dishes and fine dining. The Purple Parrot is open for lunch and dinner weekdays, Saturday dinner, and Sunday lunch at 3810 Hardy Street. Contact (601) 264-0657.

FESTIVALS AND EVENTS

Hubfest is a family community festival and features live entertainment, local food, children's activities, concerts, and arts and crafts in downtown Hattiesburg. The festival attracts hundreds of vendors and thousands of visitors from across Mississippi and several other states. Hubfest has been a Hattiesburg tradition since 1986 and is held in late March. Contact (601) 298-7500.

FestivalSouth is a multi-genre arts and music festival held in downtown Hattiesburg in June. The music includes classical, blues, jazz, gospel, and Broadway events. A variety of art including crafts and sculpture exhibits can be seen and even ballet is featured at this multi-week event. Activities for children and families are also offered. Contact (601) 296-7475.

COLLINS

HISTORY AND ATTRACTIONS

The charming town of Collins traces its history back to the early 1800's and grew as a sawmill and railroad town. Collins is now the county seat of Covington County and is located 24 miles northwest of Hattiesburg on Highway 49 in southeast Mississippi. Collins is also 63 miles southeast of Jackson from Highway 49.

One of the best waterparks in South Mississippi is located in Collins. **Grand Paradise Waterpark** is open from May to September and is located at 50 Grandview Drive in Collins. The park features seven acres of water themed attractions including four large water slides, a lazy river, splash pools, cabanas for rent, and food options. Contact (601) 765-8118 for more information.

Located just east of Collins, **Mitchell Farms** is one of the top Agritourism destinations in South Mississippi. Mitchell Farms offers an outing of family fun at the **Pumpkin Patch** during the month of October. A variety of activities are offered at the farm for children including wagon ride tours, corn mazes, pumpkin patches, and farm animal interaction. Night mazes and bonfire reservations are also offered. Mitchell Farms is located at 650 Leaf River Church Road in Collins. Contact (601) 606-0762.

The **Mississippi Peanut Festival**, complete with a Harvest King and Queen competition, food vendors, and children's activities is held annually in October at Mitchell Farms, attracting many visitors. Mitchell Farms is located at 650 Leaf River Church Road. Contact (601) 765-8609 or (601) 765-8033.

Famous residents of Collins include rock musician **Dale Houston**, actors **Dana Andrews** and **Gerald McRaney**, football stars **Steve McNair** and **Correll Buckhalter**, basketball star **Randolph Keys**, and baseball star **Billy Hamilton**. Tourist information and maps are available at the Covington County Chamber of Commerce in Collins at 500 Komo Street. Contact (601) 765-6012. For dining options in Collins, try **Morgan's on Main** at 305 Main Street for a family restaurant with southern style food. Hours: Sun.-Wed. 10:30-2:30 P.M., Thu.-Sat. 10:30-9 P.M. Contact (601) 765-2220.

The **Okatoma Festival** in Collins offers arts and crafts, food, street vendors, live entertainment, canoeing and kayaking competitions, children's activities, and a 5K run. The Okatoma Festival has been an annual tradition in Collins since 1989 as thousands of visitors accumulate on Main Street. The Okatoma Festival is held in early May. Contact (601) 765-6012.

COLUMBIA

First settled in the early 1800's, Columbia was incorporated in 1819 and became the fourth city in Mississippi. Located on the banks of the Pearl River in south Mississippi, Columbia served as the temporary capital of Mississippi from November 1821 until 1822 when the permanent capital was selected at Jackson. Historic Main Street in Columbia is filled with a variety of locally owned stores and shops. Columbia is the hometown of football legend **Walter Payton** and a life-sized bronze statue of Payton stands at the football field of Columbia High School at 1009 Broad Street. Contact (601) 731-3999. Columbia is located 30 miles west of Hattiesburg on Highway 98.

ATTRACTIONS IN COLUMBIA

The **Hugh White Mansion** was the home of former Mississippi Governor Hugh White. Built in 1925, the mansion is considered the finest example of Spanish Colonial Revival architecture in Mississippi and is listed with the National Register of Historic Places. The mansion is located north of Columbia on Hugh White Memorial Highway (Highway 13). Tours are available by appointment only. Contact (601) 736-1763.

The **John Ford House** is the oldest frontier-style structure in the Pearl River Valley and was built in 1805 by Reverend John Ford, an early settler of the area. The home was purchased by the Marion County Historical Society in 1962 and was preserved in its original condition. The elevated frontier style home is listed with the National Register of Historic Places and tours of the home are available to the public by appointment. The home is located 20 miles south of Columbia near Sandy Hook from Highway 35. Contact (601) 731-3999.

The beautiful **Marion County Courthouse** located in Columbia was constructed in the early 1900's and is a Mississippi Landmark. The building is surrounded by a courthouse square and features Classical Revival, Colonial Revival, and Italianate style architecture. The courthouse is located at 250 Broad Street. Tourist information for the Columbia area can be found at the **Marion County Development Partnership** at 412 Courthouse Square. Contact (601) 736-6385. For dining options in Columbia, try **Second Street Bean** for a nice lunch stop at 321 Second Street and enjoy coffee, sandwiches, salads, and desserts. Hours: 8-5 P.M. Mon.-Fri., Wed. 9-5 P.M. Contact (601) 444-9299.

One of Mississippi's most beautiful natural wonders, **Red Bluff** was formed as sand, soil, and clay sediment plunged 200 feet into a creek that empties into the Pearl River. Known as Mississippi's Little Grand Canyon, the erosional process is continuing and has already destroyed a section of Highway 587 twice. The highway has since been rerouted. **As of June 2014, the road leading to the highway has been closed.** The bluff is located on private property and hiking inside the bluff is prohibited, however the bluff can be easily seen from Highway 587. The bluff is located about nine miles northwest of Columbia near Morgantown. Contact (601) 731-3999 for more information.

PICAYUNE

HISTORY

Picayune is located in south Mississippi and is the largest city in Pearl River County. Picayune is 63 miles southwest of Hattiesburg, 50 miles northeast of New Orleans, and 50 miles northwest of Gulfport. Founded in 1904, Picayune was named by Eliza Jane Poitevent Nicholson, who was the owner and publisher of the New Orleans Daily Picayune. Nicholson named the town after the newspaper she owned, which was named after a Spanish coin. The railroad was built in 1883 and Picayune grew with the timber industry, the tung tree, and cattle farming. Picayune is 10 miles north of the NASA Stennis Space Center (see section on Waveland).

ATTRACTIONS

The **Crosby Arboretum** in Picayune is owned and operated by Mississippi State University. The arboretum is dedicated to "preserving, protecting, and displaying plants native to the Pearl River Drainage Basin ecosystem, providing environmental and botanical research opportunities, and offering cultural, scientific, and recreational programs." The arboretum displays three basic habitats found in this ecosystem: a savanna exhibit, a woodland exhibit, and an aquatic exhibit. The arboretum manages about 700 acres which include over 300 species of plants. The arboretum also has a visitor's center, gift shop, and a library. The arboretum is located at 370 Ridge Road near Interstate 59 in Picayune and admission is required. Hours are Wednesday-Sunday 9-5 P.M. Contact (601) 799-2311.

COASTAL MISSISSIPPI REGION

The Mississippi Gulf Coast region is located in south Mississippi along the Gulf of Mexico. This region contains some of the oldest European settlements inside the state of Mississippi. The Mississippi Gulf Coast has traditionally been a resort destination for the southeastern United States but also has major manufacturing industry and seafood industry. The region is also known as a destination for casinos. Two powerful hurricanes hit the region in recent history, including Hurricane Camille in 1969 and Hurricane Katrina in 2005. These hurricanes damaged many buildings in the region, but the reconstruction process has been ongoing. The region also offers several major museums focusing on the arts, science, and nature. Many recreational activities in the region are available including beach activities, boating, cruises, canoeing, kayaking, and swamp tours.

Gulfport-Biloxi International Airport provides access to the area from major cities in the United States. **Interstate 10** connects Gulfport and Biloxi to Louisiana and Alabama. Highway 49 connects Gulfport to Hattiesburg and Jackson.

BILOXI

HISTORY

Biloxi is an old city, being part of several European nations plus the Native American history before European settlement. The Native American history began as early as 8000 B.C. and continued after the Europeans arrived. In 1699, Sieur d'Iberville and a group of French explorers settled at the site of present day Biloxi. The settlement was named after the Biloxi Indians, who were living here when the French explorers arrived.

Biloxi grew in the early 1700's and the capital of French Louisiana was moved to Biloxi in 1720. Three years later, the capital was moved to New Orleans. In 1763, all French territory east of the Mississippi came under English control. In 1779, the Mississippi coastal region became part of Spain. By 1812, Biloxi was part of the United States.

After Mississippi statehood began in 1817, Biloxi grew as a southern resort destination. The Civil War period of the 1860's was a difficult time for Biloxi but the city managed to endure. The establishment of the railroad in the 1870's helped establish the local seafood industry and was a major boost to Biloxi. Biloxi was considered one of the top seafood industries in the world by 1900. The establishment of an air force base in the mid-20th century also was a boost to the Biloxi economy. In 1969, Hurricane Camille caused major destruction but Biloxi slowly rebuilt. The addition of the casino industry in the early 1990's was another boost for the city. Hurricane Katrina in 2005 caused serious damage, but Biloxi slowly recovered.

ATTRACTIONS

The **Biloxi Visitors Center** opened in 2011 and offers information about Biloxi attractions and also serves as a museum. The center features many multi-media exhibits which tell the story of Biloxi. A gift shop is located inside the center along with a theater showing a 10-minute film about the city of Biloxi. The center is located at 1050 Beach Boulevard and next to the Biloxi lighthouse. The center is open daily 8-5 P.M. and Sunday 10-4 P.M. Contact (228) 374-3105 or (800) 245-6943. The **Mississippi Gulf Coast Regional Convention and Visitors Bureau** also offers tourist information about the region and is located at 2350 Beach Boulevard. Contact (228) 896-6699.

RECREATIONAL ACTIVITIES

Many beach vendors are available in Biloxi which offer jet skiing, parasailing, kayaks, aqua-cycles, hydro-cycles, umbrellas and beach chairs. Boat rides and cruises are also available.

Some have said that the beach water at Biloxi looks brown or dirty. The fact is that Biloxi beach and the Mississippi Coast are shielded by the barrier islands of Gulf Coast National Seashore. These islands cause the beach to be shallow and therefore have sandy or silty water. However, the water is not dirty. If not satisfied with the main beaches, make the short boat ride to Ship Island or one of the other islands and the water will appear cleaner.

HISTORICAL ATTRACTIONS

The most iconic landmark symbol of Biloxi and the region is the **Biloxi Lighthouse**. Located at U.S. Highway 90 and Porter Avenue, the lighthouse was completed in 1848. Made of cast iron and standing 64 feet tall, the lighthouse has endured many storms and hurricanes. The lighthouse has been restored after each storm and was recently reopened in 2010 after restoration was complete from damage caused by Hurricane Katrina. Tours are available and admission is charged. Contact (228) 374-3105.

Memorials to victims of **Hurricanes Camille and Katrina** are located in Biloxi. The Camille Memorial is located at the Episcopal Church of the Redeemer at 1904 Popps Ferry Road and the Katrina Memorial is located at Biloxi Town Green at 710 Beach Boulevard. Many trees damaged by Hurricane Katrina have been carved into beautiful wooden sculptures representing egrets, seagulls, pelicans, dolphins, fishes and a variety of wildlife. These sculptures can be seen along Highway 90 and were carved in 2007 mostly by Florida native Marlin Miller and Mississippi sculptor Dayton Scoggins. These sculptures are viewed and photographed by many visitors today. Contact (228) 374-3105 for more information.

The **Historic Business District** in Biloxi is home to shops and restaurants and is centered around Main Street, Water Street, Caillavet Street, and Howard Avenue. The **Saenger Theater** at 170 Reynoir Street was constructed in 1928 and offers performing arts events. Contact (228) 435-6290.

Beauvoir was the last home of Jefferson Davis, the President of the Confederate States of America during the American Civil War of 1861 to 1865. Built in 1852 by James Brown, Davis owned the home from 1877 to his death in 1899. The home contains a Presidential library, museum, historic cemetery, and a gift shop. Beauvoir is located at 2244 Beach Boulevard and admission is charged. Hours: Daily 9-5 P.M. Contact (228) 388-4400.

The **Old Brick House** is located on a site granted by the Spanish to Jean Baptiste Carquote in 1790. The home was built around 1850 and was the residence of Mayor John L. Henley, who led the defense against the Union fleet in September 1861. The home was originally restored after the mid-20th century by the Biloxi Garden Club after years of neglect. The house is located at 622 Bayview Drive on the scenic Back Bay of

81

Biloxi. The home was heavily damaged during Hurricane Katrina, but was restored in 2011. Contact (228) 435-6121 for more information.

White Pillars is a beautifully restored two-story mansion built in 1905 with four front columns and a porch. The mansion housed an upscale restaurant for 20 years but the restaurant closed in 1989. A renovation began in 2012 and the mansion is currently being marketed for an upscale restaurant. White Pillars is located at 1696 Beach Boulevard. Contact (228) 374-3105 for more information.

The **White House Hotel** is located near the scenic view of Biloxi beach. The hotel began as a smaller house built in the late 1800's by Walter and Cora White. Walter White was a lawyer and the couple used the hotel to financially support the family. Eventually the Whites decided to start a boarding house and gradually expanded the home in the early 1900's. The hotel grew into a three story building with columns, porches, and a second floor balcony. The hotel was considered the "Crown Jewel of the Mississippi Coast by the 1920's. After Cora White's death in 1934, the hotel was sold to businessman Jimmie Love in 1940. Love continued the tradition of the hotel for three more decades until he retired and sold the hotel in 1971. Afterward, a series of owners could not keep the hotel up to par and deterioration began for several decades. Sadly in 1988, the doors of the hotel were permanently closed after bankruptcy filings. However, the hotel has recently been renovated to its former glory by new owners and opened for business in 2014. The White House Hotel is located at 1230 Beach Boulevard. Contact (228) 233-1230.

The **Biloxi City Hall** building stands three stories tall and was completed in 1908 as the U.S. Post Office, Federal Courthouse, and Customs House. Designed by James Knox Taylor in the Classical Revival style, the building frame is composed of steel construction and the exterior is composed completely of gray Italian marble. The building has been assured to last 1,000 years. The building exterior features six front columns on top of five arches on the first floor. The building became City Hall in 1960 after a land swap with the federal government and the Biloxi School Board. The building is listed on the National Register of Historic Places and was called "the finest documented building in Mississippi" by the Register. City Hall is located at 216 Lameuse Street. Contact (228) 374-3105.

The **St. Michael's Catholic Church** building was constructed in 1964 and features a unique cylindrical design with an oyster shell roof. Vertical stained glass windows grace the exterior and interior of the church. The distinctive style structure is easily seen from Highway 90 in Biloxi. The church was damaged by Hurricane Katrina but survived while surrounding buildings did not. The church is located at 177 1st Street. Contact (228) 435-5579.

CASINOS

Beau Rivage Resort and Casino is a 24-hour gaming casino with 1,740 rooms, table games, slot machines, live poker, live entertainment, restaurants, golf, shopping, and bars. Beau Rivage is located at 875 Beach Boulevard. Contact (228) 386-7111 or (888) 567-6667.

Hard Rock Casino offers 326 rooms, slots, table games, and five restaurants including Ruth's Chris Steak House and Hard Rock Café. Hard Rock Casino also offers a spa and fitness center, retail shops, and live entertainment. Hard Rock Casino is located at 777 Beach Boulevard. Contact (228) 374-7625 or (877) 877-6256.

Palace Casino is the only smoke-free casino on the Mississippi Gulf Coast and offers hotel rooms and suites, gaming, and championship golf along with restaurants including Mignon's Steaks and Seafood fine dining restaurant. Palace Casino is located at 158 Howard Avenue. Contact (228) 432-8888 or (800) 725-2239.

MUSEUMS AND ATTRACTIONS

Dedicated to promoting and preserving the legacy of Mississippi master potter George Ohr, the **Ohr-O'Keefe Museum of Art** is housed in a series of pods or curved stainless steel buildings. The museum is one of the most popular in the region and receives great reviews from visitors. The museum collections include a permanent collection and exhibitions of artwork, ceramics, and photographs. George Ohr (1857-1918) was known as the "Mad Potter of Biloxi" and is known for his ceramic artwork. Ohr is considered a pioneer in the modernist art movement and his work has been displayed in museums across the United States including the Metropolitan Museum of Art in New York City. Admission is charged to the museum, which is located at 386 Beach Boulevard. Hours: Tue.-Sun. 10-5 P.M. Contact (228) 374-5547.

The **Maritime and Seafood Industry Museum** was established in 1986 to preserve and interpret the maritime history and heritage of Biloxi and the Mississippi Gulf Coast. The museum contains a variety of exhibits focusing on the process of collecting seafood and boat building. A new museum location will open in August 2014 at 115 East 1st Street and admission is required. Hours: Tue.-Sat. 9-4:30 P.M., Sun. 12-4 P.M. Contact (228) 435-6320.

The **Craftsmen's Guild of Mississippi** opened the **Mississippi Crafts Center** in Biloxi in 2012. The center features handcrafted items by guild members. The center gives guild members another venue for showcasing and selling their craft, as well as a place in south Mississippi for tourists and locals to find extraordinary gifts. Located inside the **Slay House**, one of Biloxi's oldest existing structures, the center is part of the newly formed Rue Magnolia Arts District. The center is located at 128 Rue Magnolia. Hours: Mon.-Sat. 10-5 P.M. Contact (228) 207-0357.

The **Mississippi Coast Coliseum** hosts many sports and entertainment events including professional hockey, rodeos, and concerts. The coliseum is located at 2350 Beach Boulevard in Biloxi. Contact (228) 594-3700.

The **D'Iberville Promenade** is a 700,000 square foot shopping center offering major nationally known stores. The center is located at 3821 Promenade Parkway at the intersection of Interstate 10 and Highway 15. Hours: Mon.-Sat. 10-9 P.M. and Sun. 12-6 P.M.

DINING IN BILOXI

Mary Mahoney's Old French House features one of the most distinguished restaurants in Biloxi. The restaurant is located inside a home built in 1737 by Louis Frasier when Biloxi was a French town. The home features hand-made brick, cypress wooden columns, tall ceilings, a wine cellar, and a slate roof characteristic of New Orleans. French Governor Jean Baptiste Bienville commanded the entire Louisiana Territory from this home. A variety of nationalities lived in the home as Biloxi came under control of the French, Spanish, and English. The home was purchased in 1962 by Mary Mahoney and her family and the restaurant was established. For over half a century, the restaurant has hosted Presidents, celebrities, dignitaries, and many others. The restaurant setting features a beautiful courtyard and large oak trees. A 2,000 year old oak tree named "Patriarch" is adjacent to the restaurant. Mary Mahoney's is located at 110 Rue Magnolia. The menu features shrimp, crab, oyster, flounder, lobster, a selection of steaks and signature dishes. Hours: Mon.-Sat. 11-10 P.M. Contact (228) 374-0163.

Half Shell Oyster House is located at 125 Lameuse Street in Downtown Biloxi inside a historic two-story bank building. The restaurant features oysters, a variety of seafood, fish selections, steaks, pasta, burgers, and sandwiches. The restaurant is open daily 11-10 P.M. and Fri.-Sat. 11-11 P.M. Contact (228) 432-5050. Half Shell Oyster

House also has a location in Gulfport at 2500 13th Street inside the Historic Kremer Building.

Ole Biloxi Schooner is located at 871 Howard Avenue and offers seafood and po-boy sandwiches. Seafood items include fried shrimp, oysters, crab, and fish. Hours: Mon. 10:30-3 P.M., Wed.-Thu. 7 A.M.-8 P.M., Fri.-Sat. 7 A.M.-9 P.M. Contact (228) 435-8071.

FESTIVALS AND EVENTS

The **Coliseum Crawfish Music Festival** is held in Biloxi in middle to late April at the coliseum and has been a tradition since 1992. The two-week festival features a variety of music performances, a variety of food vendors, a crawfish cook off, arts and crafts vendors, amusement rides, and children's activities. The coliseum is located at 2350 Beach Boulevard. Contact (228) 594-3700.

The **Biloxi Seafood Festival** is held in middle September and features a variety of seafood dishes, arts and crafts, children's activities, and live music performances. A tradition since 1981, the annual festival attracts thousands of visitors and is a Southeast Tourism Society Top 20 Fall Event. The festival is held at Biloxi Town Green at 710 Beach Boulevard. Contact (228) 604-0014.

Crusin' the Coast is an annual week-long event held in October on the Mississippi coast where over 5,000 classic, antique, and hot rod automobiles are showcased along the beautiful beachside highway. The event features drag races, sock hops, swap meets, food vendors, and live music and entertainment. Visitors from over 40 states and several countries register their classic vehicles at the event. Crusin' the Coast has been a tradition since 1996 and has been recognized by the Southeast Tourism Society and several regional and national organizations. The event also makes stops in Biloxi, Bay St. Louis, D'Iberville, Gulfport, and Ocean Springs. Contact (228) 385-3847.

The annual **Biloxi St. Patrick's Day Parade** is held in March and has been a tradition since 1978. The parade features bands, bagpipers, leprechauns, military units, Irish themed floats, an Irish derby and a 5K Run. Another more recent event held in conjunction with the parade is the annual **Grillin' on the Green**, which features a large barbeque competition, arts and crafts vendors, live entertainment, and children's activities on the Biloxi Town Green. Contact (228) 435-6339.

The **Mississippi Gulf Coast Carnival Association Mardi Gras Parade** is held in downtown Biloxi and is the largest Mardi Gras parade on the Mississippi Coast. Held in March on Fat Tuesday, the parade has been a tradition since 1908 and was the first Mardi Gras parade in Biloxi. While the first parade only had 17 floats, the parade has grown over the last century and today has over 100 floats. The colorful floats travel down the street as thousands of visitors enjoy the festivities of this family friendly parade. Contact (228) 432-8806.

The annual **Coast Coliseum Summer Fair** is a family friendly ten day event held in Biloxi in June on the grounds of the Mississippi Coast Coliseum. The fair offers a variety of amusement rides, live music, shows, contests, and entertainment. The fair has been named a Top 20 Event by the Southeast Tourism Society and has been a tradition since 1986. The coliseum is located at 2350 Beach Boulevard. Contact (228) 594-3700.

GULFPORT

Gulfport was incorporated as a city in 1898 and shares a border with Biloxi to the east. Gulfport was founded by William Hardy and Joseph Jones, who were railroad industry executives in the late 19th century and early 20th century. The Port of Gulfport and access to the beach allowed the city to grow rapidly as a business and tourist center. Hurricanes

Camille and Katrina severely damaged the city but reconstruction has continued since. Gulfport is now the largest populated city in the region and the second largest city in Mississippi.

MUSEUMS

The **Institute for Marine Mammals Studies** is a non-profit organization established in 1984 for the purposes of public education, conservation, and research on marine mammals in the wild and under human care. Tours of the facility allow visitors to explore the interactive museum, which features sea creatures such as stingrays, sharks, horseshoe crabs, fish, blue crabs, sea stars, and sea urchins. Visitors will also find a shark tooth in the fossil dig to keep as a souvenir. In addition, tropical birds and reptiles are part of the presentations. Dolphin presentations are the most popular attraction and are available to the public by reservation only and for a fee. The institute is located at 10801 Dolphin Lane. Contact (228) 896-9182 for more information and for reservations.

The **Mississippi Gulf Coast Regional Convention and Visitors Bureau** offers tourist information about the region and is located at 2350 Beach Boulevard in Biloxi. Contact (228) 896-6699 for Gulfport and regional tourist information.

Lynn Meadows Discovery Center is a popular children's museum which features a variety of indoor and outdoor interactive exhibits designed for children and families. The indoor portion contains 15,000 square feet of exhibit space. The center receives great reviews from visitors and has been ranked with the top children's museums in the United States. The center is located at 246 Dolan Avenue in Gulfport and admission is charged. Hours: Tue.-Sat. 10-5 P.M., Sun. 12-5 P.M. Contact (228) 897-6039.

RECREATION

Gulf Islands Waterpark is the top water park and family attraction on the Mississippi Gulf Coast. The park features 18 acres of water slides and water themed attractions for children and adults including a lazy river. The park also hosts celebrity performances. The park is located near Interstate 10 and Highway 49 and is open from May to Labor Day. Hours are Sun.-Thu. 10-6 P.M., Fri.-Sat. 10-7 P.M. Contact (228) 328-1266 for more information.

The **Harrison County Fairgrounds** include a 32,000 square foot multipurpose facility that hosts a variety of sports and entertainment events including rodeos, horse shows, motor sports, and dog shows. The fairgrounds are located at 15321 County Farm Road in Gulfport. Contact (228) 832-8620.

Lunch and Dinner Cruises are available at the **Port of Gulfport** along with charter cruises. Contact (228) 896-6699 or (888) 467-4853.

SHIP ISLAND AND FORT MASSACHUSETTS

Ship Island is one of four barrier islands which are part of **Gulf Islands National Seashore**. The island is located about 11 miles south of Gulfport and Biloxi. The mostly undeveloped island features great beaches which are popular with tourists and offers a break from the busy mainland beaches. Bird viewing and hiking are also popular on the island along with dolphin sighting. Ferry boat rides to Ship Island are available for a fee.

The island features **Fort Massachusetts,** which was built on Ship Island for national defense in 1868. Both domestic and foreign powers recognized the strategic significance of the natural deep water harbor on the north side of the island. After lengthy debate, fort construction began

89

in the summer of 1859. Storms, disease, climate, isolation and the Civil War made construction on this remote barrier island a challenge. The fort has not only withstood actions of war but also the effects of time and neglect. The devastating and powerful Hurricane Camille of 1969 and Katrina in 2005 washed over and through the building but failed to significantly undermine or damage the structure. Ship Island excursions are available from Gulfport Yacht Harbor from March to October. Contact (228) 864-1014 for more information.

SHOPPING IN GULFPORT

Gulfport Premium Outlets offers 70 nationally known outlet store brands with discounted prices and is the only outlet shopping center on the Mississippi Gulf Coast. The Outlets are located at the intersection of Interstate 10 and Highway 49 at Exit 34. Hours: Mon.-Sat. 10-9 P.M., Sun. 11-6 P.M. Contact (228) 867-6100.

DINING IN GULFPORT

Salute Italian Restaurant is located at 1712 15th Street. Hours: Mon.-Sat. 11-9 P.M., Sun. 11-8 P.M. Contact (228) 864-2500.

Lookout Steakhouse is a family restaurant located in downtown Gulfport at 1301 26th Avenue. Hours: Mon.-Sat. 11-9 P.M., Sun. 11-8 P.M. Contact (228) 248-0555.

Tony's Brick Oven Pizzeria is located at 2417 14th Street and is open daily 11-10 P.M. (Sun. 11-9 P.M.) Contact (228) 868-9877.

FESTIVALS AND EVENTS

The **Gulf Coast Yacht and Boat Super Show** is the largest outdoor boat show on the Gulf Coast. The show is held in Gulfport in early April and attracts over 26,000 visitors from 18 states and three countries. Over 600 boats are showcased from a variety of nationally known brands. Accessory vendors at the show feature related merchandise including engines, electronics, art, apparel, docks, and more. The show is located at Gulfport Harbor at 1120 20th Avenue.

The annual **Gulfport Music Festival** has grown to be the largest music event on the Mississippi Coast. The weekend festival features today's hottest nationally-known artists representing a variety of genres of music. The festival also offers food booths and is held in Jones Park in Gulfport in early May. Contact (228) 388-2001.

LONG BEACH

Long Beach was incorporated as a town in 1905 and shares a border with Gulfport to the east. Long Beach began as an agricultural town, specifically with the radish crop and logging. More recently tourism has increased in Long Beach because of the proximity to the beachfront. Destruction from Hurricane Katrina has slowed growth but the outlook is positive. **Friendship Oak** is a 500 year old oak tree located at 730 East Beach Boulevard in Long Beach on the campus of the University of Southern Mississippi Gulf Park. Friendship Oak is one of the most photographed landmarks on the Mississippi Coast. The tree is 59 feet tall, has a five foot nine inch trunk diameter, and a 155 foot wide foliage spread. Contact (228) 865-4500.

FESTIVALS AND EVENTS

The **Mississippi Gulf Coast Kite Festival** is an annual event held at Long Beach harbor in late April. The festival features children's games, kite making, sand castle making, and food vendors. The festival is a Southeast Tourism Society Top 20 Event and has been a tradition since 1989. Contact (228) 604-0014.

PASS CHRISTIAN

HISTORY

Pass Christian is a city located in Harrison County west of Long Beach and faces St. Louis Bay. Chartered in 1848, the city has a rich history and several festivals are held here. Pass Christian was discovered in 1699 by French Canadian explorers shortly after a colony was established at Biloxi. The city was named after the nearby deep water pass and after Nicholas Christian de L'Adnier, who lived on Cat Island in 1746. The Pass Christian area was under the rule of the French, the English, the Spanish, and was part of an independent republic before being annexed into the United States.

Pass Christian emerged as a small fishing commercial harbor and trading center. The town also was a famous resort prior to the Civil War, as wealthy New Orleans residents built a row of historic mansions along the shoreline. The **Southern Yacht Club** was established in 1849, which was the first Yacht Club in the South and the second in the United States. The club moved to New Orleans in 1857, but a new yacht club was established in Pass Christian in the mid-20th century.

Pass Christian was attacked by Union forces during the Civil War and the **Battle of Pass Christian**. The USS *Massachusetts* began shelling Pass Christian in a surprise move as the Union forces were expected to attack Biloxi. The unprepared town of Pass Christian quickly surrendered and Union forces soon left.

The **Pass Christian Historic District** contains many antebellum homes and historic buildings along the shoreline. Contact (228) 452-7254 for more information. The **Mississippi Gulf Coast Chamber of Commerce** can also provide tourist information at (228) 604-0105. Pass Christian has recovered substantially from Hurricane Katrina and the future is positive as new developments emerge.

The **Oak Crest Mansion Inn** is a historic luxury bed and breakfast featuring five suites, antiques, and a full breakfast. The two-floor building was built in 1920 and is located on 12 acres with landscaped gardens at 5267 Menge Avenue. Contact (228) 452-5677.

For dining options in Pass Christian, try the **Pirate's Cove** for po-boy sandwiches and burgers at 116 Market Street. Hours: Sun.-Thu. 10:30-8 P.M., Fri.-Sat. 10:30-9 P.M. Contact (228) 452-4721.

FESTIVALS AND EVENTS

The **Pass Christian Oyster Festival** is a celebration of art, family, history and heritage, food and drink with an emphasis on oysters. The weekend festival is held in late January and features eating contests, amusement rides, live music and entertainment, arts and crafts, a boat parade, and food vendors. The annual festival has been recognized by regional and national organizations and was named a top 20 event in the Southeast. Contact (228) 222-2916.

The **Mississippi Gulf Coast Spring Pilgrimage** is a week-long event where visitors can receive complementary tours of historic homes, gardens, museums, and landmarks on the Mississippi coastal region. A different region of the coast is showcased each day. The Pilgrimage has

93

been a tradition since 1952 and is held in late March. Contact (228) 896-6699.

Art in the Pass is a two-day annual arts festival held in Pass Christian in early April. The festival attracts many talented artists and thousands of visitors to view a variety of art including paintings, photography, sculptures, pottery, and jewelry. Free seafood and cooking demonstrations are offered at the festival. The festival has been a tradition since 1997. Contact (228) 452-3315.

Christmas in the Pass is an annual event held in early December in Pass Christian and features the lighting of the Christmas tree, the arrival of Santa Claus, local music, children's activities, a holiday parade, craft and food vendors, and a 5K run. The event has been a tradition since 1985 and has been named a Southeast Tourism Society top 20 event. Contact (228) 604-0014.

BAY ST. LOUIS

Bay St. Louis is located on St. Louis Bay and inside Hancock County. This coastal city has a unique charm and has been recognized by national publications. Bay St. Louis features several historic sites, festivals, and attractions for visitors. The **Mississippi West Coast-Hancock County Tourism Development Bureau** can provide tourist information and is located at 1928 Depot Way in Bay St. Louis. Contact (228) 463-9222 or (800) 466-9048.

The **Bay BridgeFest** is an award-winning festival held in September to celebrate the re-opening of Bay Bridge after being destroyed by Hurricane Katrina. The three-day festival is held in **Old Town Bay St. Louis** at Main Street and Second Street. The festival features live music performances, art, craft, and food vendors, entertainment for all ages, and a 5K run. Contact (228) 467-9048.

The **Historic Bay St. Louis Depot** is a uniquely restored two-story train depot built in 1928 in the Mission architectural style. The building is listed with the National Register of Historic Places and includes a visitor center and a museum featuring Mardi Gras costumes. Contact (228) 463-9222. Other historic buildings in Bay St. Louis include **City Hall**, which features a two-story building with Classical Revival architecture and is located at 300 Second Street. The **Hancock County Courthouse** is a two-story building featuring Greek Revival style architecture and is located at 150 Main Street. The **Kate Lobrano House** is an 1890's Victorian cottage that includes a large collection of old Hancock County photography and is located at 108 Cue Street. The **Hancock County Historical Society** is also part of the house, which is open weekdays from 10 A.M. to 3 P.M. Contact (228) 467-4090.

DINING IN BAY ST. LOUIS

Cannella Restaurant is located at 1113 Highway 90 in Bay St. Louis and serves German, Italian, and International cuisine. Hours: Wed. 11-2 P.M., 6-8:30 P.M., Thu.-Sat. 11-8:30 P.M., Sun. 12-7:30 P.M. Contact (228) 467-4110.

WAVELAND

The city of Waveland is located west of Bay St. Louis and inside Hancock County. Hurricane Katrina severely damaged Waveland and destroyed all of Buccaneer State Park's structures, but since then most have been rebuilt. **Buccaneer State Park** is located in a natural setting of large moss-draped oaks, marshlands, and the beachfront. The park includes 200 premium campsites with full amenities, a waterpark, nature trails, and picnic pavilions. The park is located at 1150 South Beach Boulevard. Contact (228) 467-3822.

The **Mississippi West Coast Hancock County Tourism Development Bureau** is located at 1928 Depot Way in Bay St. Louis and can provide tourist information. Contact (228) 463-9222 or (800) 466-9048.

The **Infinity Science Center** is a joint effort between the NASA Stennis Space Center, Leo W. Seal, and others to form a non-profit foundation with the goal of raising the funds to create a science center that would become a world class attraction of Hancock County and the state of Mississippi. Exhibits include the OMEGA Flight Simulator, an F-1 rocket engine, Science on a Sphere, Space Gallery, and a tour of the Stennis Space Center, which is the largest rocket engine test facility in the United States. The center is located at Interstate 10 and Exit 2, next door to the Mississippi Welcome Center. Admission is charged at the center, which is open Monday through Friday, 10-4 P.M. Contact (228) 533-9025.

DINING

For dining options in Waveland, try the **West End Restaurant**, which is located at 635 Highway 90. West End serves New Orleans cuisine, seafood, salads, burgers, pasta, and steaks. Hours: Tue.-Sat., 11-9 P.M., Fri.-Sat., 11-9:30 P.M. Contact (228) 466-5225.

FESTIVALS AND EVENTS

WaveFest is an annual event held in Waveland that features live music, activities, a pirate costume contest, craft and food vendors, a 5K run and more. WaveFest is held in October and has been a tradition since 1990. Contact (228) 467-0855.

OCEAN SPRINGS

HISTORY

Ocean Springs is the site of the first European settlement in Mississippi, which occurred in 1699 on the eastern shore of Biloxi Bay. **Fort Maurepas** was built in present day Ocean Springs by Frenchmen Pierre Le Moyne d'Iberville and his brother Jean Baptiste de Bienville. Hurricane Katrina brought damage to the city, but reconstruction has been ongoing. Today, Ocean Springs has a vibrant arts community and is home to many galleries and art studios. Ocean Springs also has a historic downtown featuring galleries, shops, and streets lined with oak trees. In addition, a diverse selection of restaurants can be found in the city, particularly on or near **Government Street**. Many restaurants are also located along Highway 90.

The **Ocean Springs Chamber of Commerce** can provide tourist information at 1000 Washington Avenue. Contact (228) 875-4424. **Fort Maurepas Park** in Ocean Springs is the site of the first European settlement in Mississippi and is located at 499 Front Beach Drive. Contact (228) 875-4236.

MUSEUMS

The **Walter Anderson Museum of Art** in Ocean Springs has been open since 1991 and is dedicated to promoting the works of Ocean Springs native Walter Inglis Anderson (1903-1965). The museum also focuses on Anderson's two brothers and includes paintings, pottery, and ceramics. The permanent collection focuses on the works of the Anderson brothers while various changing exhibitions showcase other artists throughout the year. The museum is one of the top art museums in the region and receives great reviews from visitors. Admission is charged to enter the museum, which is located at 510 Washington Avenue. Hours: Mon.-Sat. 9:30-4:30 P.M., Sun. 12:30-4:30 P.M. Contact (228) 872-3164.

The **Mary O'Keefe Cultural Center for Arts and Education** is located inside the historic Ocean Springs School, a beautiful two story brick building. The center is named after Mary O'Keefe, the first female public school superintendent in Mississippi. The center offers a variety of programs and facilities for the arts. The center offers performing arts, a music studio, visual arts and art galleries. Some of the performances require admission. The center is located at 1600 Government Street. Hours: Mon.-Sat. 10-6 P.M. Contact (228) 818-2878.

FESTIVALS AND EVENTS

The annual **Peter Anderson Arts and Crafts Festival** is Mississippi's largest fine arts festival, with over 400 artists, craftsmen, music and food vendors, and over 100,000 visitors. The weekend festival was created to honor master potter Peter Anderson and has grown into one of the largest arts festivals in the Southeast. Surrounding the festival area in downtown Ocean Springs are over 150 shops, restaurants, and local galleries. The festival has been a tradition since 1978 and is held in early November. The festival's awards include Festival of the Year for the Southeast by the Southeast Tourism Society and recognition from many other regional and national publications. Contact (228) 875-4424.

DINING IN OCEAN SPRINGS

The Shed is an iconic juke joint that combines barbeque with blues music and is extremely popular with locals and tourists. The Shed features wood burning pits cooking great barbeque, old school blues music, and antique items displayed everywhere for a truly unique experience. The Shed is located at 7501 Highway 57. Hours: Tue.-Thu. 11-9 P.M., Fri.-Sat. 11-10 P.M., Sun. 11-9 P.M. Contact (228) 875-9590.

Phoenicia Gourmet Restaurant serves Greek and Mediterranean cuisine and is located at 1223 Government Street. Hours: Mon.-Thu. 7 A.M.-9 P.M., Fri.-Sat. 7 A.M.-10 P.M., Sun. 7 A.M.-2:30 P.M. Contact (228) 875-0603.

Leo's Wood Fired Pizza is located at 1107 Government Street. Hours: Sun.-Thu. 11-9 P.M., Fri.-Sat. 11-10 P.M. Contact (228) 872-7283.

Anthony's Steak & Seafood is located at 1217 Washington Avenue. Hours: Tue.-Thu. 5-9 P.M., Fri.-Sat. 5-9:30. Contact (228) 872-4564.

Bayview Gourmet serves breakfast and lunch and features omelets, wraps, sandwiches, and salads. Bayview Gourmet is located at 1010 Robinson Street. Hours: Tue.-Sun. 7:30-2:30 P.M. Contact (228) 875-4252.

PASCAGOULA

HISTORY

Pascagoula is the largest city on the Mississippi coast east of Biloxi. Known for its shipbuilding industry, Pascagoula features oak trees covered with Spanish moss, antebellum structures, and a coastal fishing village atmosphere. Pascagoula was a small fishing village until World War II when the shipbuilding industry emerged. The industry continues strong today. Pascagoula also has a major oil refinery and other related industries. A new modern museum is in the planning stages for Pascagoula as of 2014 that would focus on the shipbuilding industry in Pascagoula and the region.

The Jackson County Chamber of Commerce is located at 720 Krebs Avenue in Pascagoula. Contact (228) 762-3391. **Anchor Square** is located in downtown Pascagoula at 303 Delmas Avenue and offers shops, restaurants, and galleries inside 16 cottages in addition to a boardwalk and a town green.

Built in 1859, the **Round Island Lighthouse** once was located off the coast of Pascagoula and was overturned by Hurricane Georges in 1998. The base of the lighthouse was moved to the mainland in 2010 and was restored to its original condition. Today, the lighthouse stands in downtown Pascagoula and is a gateway to the city. Contact (228) 938-6639.

DINING IN PASCAGOULA

For dining options in Pascagoula, **Bozo's Grocery** is located at 2012 Ingalls Avenue and offers seafood and po-boy sandwiches in addition to a grocery store and seafood market. Hours are 8 A.M.-8 P.M. daily. Contact (228) 762-3322.

FESTIVALS AND EVENTS

The annual **Live Oak Arts Festival** is held in downtown Pascagoula in early May. The festival focuses on arts, live music, Pascagoula heritage, and the preservation of live oak trees. The festival also features specialty vendors and children's activities. Contact (228) 938-6604. Admission is free.

The annual **Zonta Arts & Crafts Festival** is Pascagoula's premier event and features arts, crafts, and food vendors, exhibit booths, an antique car show, children's activities, and free live entertainment. The festival is held in early October in downtown Pascagoula and has been a tradition since 1978. Contact (228) 229-9908. Admission is free.

The annual **Jackson County Fair** features amusement rides for all ages, arts and craft vendors, food vendors, live music and entertainment, livestock shows, and more. The week-long fair has been a Pascagoula tradition since 1921 and is held in late October. Contact (228) 762-6043. Admission is free.

The annual **Mississippi Gulf Coast Blues & Heritage Festival** is held in Pascagoula in early September. The award winning festival features well-known blues performers, food, and exhibits. The festival has been a tradition since 1991. Contact (228) 497-5493.

MOSS POINT

Moss Point was incorporated in 1901 at the junction of two rivers, the Pascagoula and the Escatawpa River. Moss Point is a beautiful city, with moss covered oak trees, magnolia and pine trees, and many other varieties of trees and flowering plants. Historic homes and churches are featured in the city, along with clear lakes and bayous. For tourism information, the **Jackson County Chamber of Commerce** is located at 720 Krebs Avenue in Pascagoula. Contact (228) 762-3391.

RECREATION

The **Escatawpa River Observatory** is located on a tall bluff near the Escatawpa River and the Mississippi Welcome Center on Interstate 10 near Moss Point. The observatory offers many birding and wildlife viewing opportunities in an environment consisting of wet pine savannah and mixed woodlands. Hours: 8-5 P.M. daily. Contact (228) 475-3384.

The **Pascagoula River Audubon Center** is a gateway to the Pascagoula River and provides visitors with a variety of opportunities for exploration of the rich flora and fauna in and around the river. The center offers boat tours by reservation, elevated boardwalks which allow visitors to view the wetland and river wildlife, along with on-site demonstrations. The center is located at 7001 Frank Griffin Road in Moss Point. Hours: Tue.-Sat. 9-4 P.M. Contact (228) 475-0825.

THE DELTA REGION OF NORTHWEST MISSISSIPPI

Northwest Mississippi is commonly referred to as "the Delta," however this region is actually part of the Mississippi River alluvial floodplain in geographic terms. The region has a unique racial, cultural, and economic history as it is one of the most fertile agricultural lands on earth. Choctaw and Chickasaw Indians inhabited the Delta region prior to European settlement. Several treaties in the 1830's gave the Indians land in Oklahoma in exchange for the land in the Delta region and European settlers came afterward. Cotton became the biggest crop in the region and many came here in the mid-1800's to build cotton plantations using slave laborers, who made up a majority of the population. The mechanization of agriculture reduced the need for laborers in the field and many left the region in the 1920's.

The **Great Migration** refers to the exodus of many African American Mississippians to the northern United States in the 20th century to places such as Chicago and Detroit. Many left for economic reasons and for better job opportunities. The Mississippi Delta region is strongly associated with Blues music and was influenced by the economic struggles of individuals living in the region, mostly among African-Americans. The Blues genre of music is being promoted as a way to display the cultural heritage of the region and to promote tourism. Several major museums are located in the region that promote the musical heritage that originated here. The Delta region is also known for its cuisine and several award-winning restaurants can be found here.

TUNICA

Tunica is a city located in northwestern Mississippi and is known as a major casino destination. Located near Memphis to the southwest, Tunica is also known as the Gateway to the Blues and the Highway 61 Mississippi Blues Trail. The city of Tunica is the county seat of Tunica County and was named after the Tunica Native Americans, who migrated to Louisiana during the Colonial Period. Tracing its history to the early 1800's, Tunica grew rapidly from the middle 1800's to the middle 1900's. After 1950, Tunica had a substantial loss of population and by 1990 was one of the poorest places in America. In 1990, casino gaming was legalized in Mississippi on the river and the coastal waters. The effect was a dramatic impact on the local economy and today there are nine casinos in Tunica. The casinos are actually located about 11 miles north of Tunica in the town of **Robinsonville**, which is inside Tunica County and along Highway 61.

ATTRACTIONS IN TUNICA

The **Gateway to the Blues Visitor Center and Museum** is located in a restored train depot (1895) and provides information to visitors including directions, events, restaurants, and attractions in the area. The visitor center will soon be home to the **Gateway to the Blues Museum**. Opening in 2014, the museum will be a key attraction for music and blues fans travelling down Highway 61. The museum will focus on the history of blues music and the role Tunica played in its development. The museum is located at 13625 Highway 61 North and is open daily. Contact (662) 363-3800 or (888) 488-6422.

The **Tunica Riverpark** is located on the bank of the Mississippi River and allows visitors to view the natural beauty of the river and the surrounding wildlife. The Riverpark features professional landscaping and sidewalks, a state of the art museum, and access to riverboat cruises, nature trails, and a gift shop. The **Mississippi River Museum** at the Riverpark features artifacts and interactive exhibits focused on history, nature, and culture. Four freshwater aquariums in the museum allow visitors to see lowland and aquatic life. The park and museum are open daily except Mondays. Hours: March-October 10-7 P.M. November-February 10-5 P.M. Contact (662) 357-0050 or (866) 517-4837.

The **Tunica Queen Riverboat** is a 400 seat luxury ship that offers a 1.5 hour sightseeing cruise and a two hour night dinner cruise. The Tunica Queen can be accessed from the Riverpark and is available March to November. The Tunica Riverpark and Tunica Queen can be found by way of Highway 61 at Casino Strip Resort Boulevard, Fitzgeralds Boulevard, and Lucky Lane. Contact (662) 363-7622 or (866) 805-3535.

The **Tunica Museum** is housed in a modern building and focuses on the history of Tunica from the Native American heritage, the Civil War period, and the building of casinos in 1992. The museum features educational exhibits, photographs, artifacts, and lectures. The museum is free and is located at One Museum Boulevard near Highway 61. Hours: Tue.-Sat. 10-5 P.M. Contact (662) 363-6631.

The **Tate House** is a 19th century log home featuring furnishings from the time period including beds, clothing, and tools. Built in 1840, the one story log home is now a museum and is the oldest structure in Tunica County. The house is located at 1014 Magnolia Street in Tunica and is available April to October. Hours: Tue.-Sat. 9-5 P.M. Contact (662) 363-6631.

The **Veterans Memorial at Rivergate Park** serves as a memorial to the men and women in uniform who have fought for America. The seven-foot tall bronze monument features three soldiers in uniform at the Veterans Memorial Plaza, which can be found at 999 River Road in downtown Tunica. Also while in downtown Tunica, a one can find a variety of charming shops and antique stores. Contact (662) 363-6611.

Tunica National is one of Mississippi's top golf and tennis venues and features a tournament-level 18 hole course designed by PGA tour player Mark McCumber. Tunica National's Pro Shop offers a variety of golf and tennis equipment and apparel inside the modern clubhouse, which also features a restaurant. An indoor, clay-court tennis facility is also available at Tunica National, which is located at One Champions Lane near Highway 61 and the casinos. Contact (662) 357-0777 or (866) 833-6331.

River Bend Links is another professional golf course near the Mississippi River and the casinos. Designed by Clyde Johnston and described as a "field of dunes," the Links incorporates a Scottish golf course design. River Bend Links also offers a restaurant and pro shop at 1205 Nine Lakes Drive. Contact (662) 363-1005.

DINING IN TUNICA

For dining options in Tunica, most of the top restaurants are located inside the casinos. One exception is the **Hollywood Café,** which is located at 1585 Old Commerce Road. One of the most recognized restaurants in the region, Hollywood Café has been open since 1969 and is known for southern cuisine, burgers, and sandwiches. Author John Grisham was a regular here before becoming famous and the café was mentioned in the novel *A Time to Kill*. The Hollywood Café was also featured in Marc Cohn's song "Walking in Memphis." Today Hollywood Café is visited by prominent politicians, celebrities, tourists, and locals. Hours: Tue.-Thu. 11-2 P.M., 4-9 P.M., Fri. 11-2 P.M., 4-10 P.M., Sat. 4-10 P.M. Contact (662) 363-1225.

CLARKSDALE

Located at the intersection of Highway 61 and Highway 49 in northwest Mississippi, Clarksdale is known for blues music and has produced many blues musicians. The world-recognized **Delta Blues Museum** was established in 1979 and features the history and significance of blues music in the Delta region. Mississippi's oldest music museum includes wax figures of Muddy Waters and the famous Muddywood Guitar along with a portion of Waters former home. The museum also includes video, photographs, music recordings, books, memorabilia, and archives of blues music and musicians. The guitars of other famous blues musicians such as B.B. King are also on display. The museum is located at One Blues Alley and admission is required. Hours: March-October: Mon.-Sat. 9-5 P.M., November-February: 10-5 P.M. Contact (662) 627-6820.

ATTRACTIONS IN CLARKSDALE

Ground Zero Blues Club is located next door to the Delta Blues Museum in historic downtown Clarksdale. Opening in 2001, the club is owned by attorney and businessman Bill Luckett, Academy Award winning actor Morgan Freeman, and Clarksdale native Howard Stovall. The club strives to showcase the best of Delta blues musicians and features both local names and nationally known performers. The club also serves a full menu of southern cooking. Ground Zero has been featured on national television stations and in national magazines, in addition to being named to the top 100 Bars and Nightclubs in America. Lunch is served Mon.-Fri. 11-2 P.M. Live music available Wed.-Sat. Contact (662) 621-9009.

The **Hopson Plantation** and commissary features antiques and artifacts associated with Mississippi Delta Blues culture. Cotton farming required a large amount of manual labor. However, in 1935 Hopson plantation became the first to use mechanized cotton pickers completely. The plantation features one of the first mechanized cotton pickers on display. At the plantation, visitors can listen to blues music, learn about the history of the Delta, and even arrange lodging accommodations. The plantation is open year-round by appointment and admission is free. Hopson Plantation is located at 8141 Old Highway 49. Contact (662) 624-5756.

FESTIVALS AND EVENTS

The **Pinetop Perkins Homecoming** is an annual celebration in Clarksdale in honor of legendary blues musician and pianist Pinetop Perkins. Perkins was one of the last great Mississippi blues musicians and continued to perform until his death in 2011 at age 97. Several blues musicians are invited to perform at the event, which is held at Hopson Commissary in October and food is available.

Clarksdale is also the hometown of author **Tennessee Williams**, who spent much of his childhood here. Tennessee Williams Park was established in honor of Williams at Clark Street and Court Street in downtown Clarksdale. Clarksdale also features several **art galleries** featuring artwork, pottery, and fine arts by local artists. For more tourism information about Clarksdale, contact the **Coahoma County Tourism Commission** at 1540 DeSoto Avenue (662) 627-7337 or (800) 626-3764.

The annual **Mississippi Delta Tennessee Williams Festival** is held in early October in Clarksdale and is sponsored by Coahoma Community College. Clarksdale is the childhood home of Tennessee Williams, who was a great American playwright and Pulitzer Prize winning author. Even though he left Mississippi as an adult, Williams' Delta childhood greatly influenced his writings and work. Each year the festival focuses on one play and scholars and experts are invited to Clarksdale to present lectures, readings, and dramatizations. The festival has been a tradition since 1993. Contact (662) 627-7337.

CLEVELAND

Cleveland traces its history back to the late 1800's as a settlement known by several names. In 1886, the town was officially named Cleveland after Grover Cleveland, the former American President. Cleveland is known as a college town, the home of **Delta State University**, which is the largest university in the region. Downtown Cleveland offers a charming variety of boutique shops and restaurants around Cotton Row and Sharpe Street. Cleveland tourism information can be found at 600 Third Street. Contact (662) 843-2712 or (800) 295-7473. **Octoberfest** is a two day festival held in downtown Cleveland in October and features a barbeque contest, food vendors, children's activities, live music, and arts and crafts. Contact (662) 843-2712.

ATTRACTIONS IN CLEVELAND

The **Bologna Performing Arts Center** provides world-class entertainment to the region and is located on the Delta State University campus. Built in 1995 with funding from the Mississippi Legislature, the center features a 1,171 seat theater, a full working stage, an orchestra lift, and a large sculpture garden outside. With a variety of performances from blues music to Broadway, the center has received awards in several major publications and is considered one of the top performing arts centers in Mississippi. The center is located near Highway 8 on campus at 1003 West Sunflower Road. Contact (662) 846-4626.

The **Fielding Wright Art Center** at Delta State University contains studio classrooms for the art department and also contains two galleries for art exhibitions and the permanent collection. The permanent collection includes original works by Salvador Dali, Kathe Kollwitz, Leonard Baskin, Marie Hull, William Hollingsworth, Walter Anderson and more. The center is named after the late Mississippi Governor Fielding Wright and is located at 1003 West Sunflower Road. Hours: Mon.-Fri. 8-5 P.M. Contact (662) 846-4720.

A **Cast of Blues** is a truly unique exhibit. Figurative sculptor Sharon McConnell has created life-size masks of 55 blues musicians which are on display at Delta State University. Originally from New England, McConnell studied art in New Mexico and focused on clay figure studies and direct casting. After discovering a love of blues music, McConnell moved to Mississippi and began creating the masks of the faces of the music in which she loved. The Cast of Blues is on display at Ewing Hall at Highway 8 and North Fifth Avenue. Contact (662) 846-4311.

The **GRAMMY® Museum** is a state of the art interactive museum which will be located on the Delta State University campus in 2015. The 20,000 square foot facility will be the first GRAMMY® museum outside of Los Angeles and will showcase Mississippi's rich musical heritage in blues, country, rock, gospel, and pop music along with famous musicians and songwriters nationwide. Contact (662) 843-2712 or (800) 295-7473.

Dockery Plantation was a 10,000 acre cotton plantation and sawmill located just east of Cleveland on Highway 8. It is here that some believe Delta Blues music began as several famous blues performers were residents at the plantation: Charlie Patton, Robert Johnson, and Howlin' Wolf. The plantation, which was founded in 1895, is listed on the National Register of Historic Places. Private tours of the plantation are available throughout the year. Contact (662) 719-1048.

Juke Joints had an important role in the development of blues music and offered a place for people to socialize, dance, and forget about their worries. A juke joint would commonly feature a juke box, a pool table, beer posters on the wall, and Christmas lights inside. Typically a small wooden building in the countryside, many juke joints existed in the Delta region in the past but today few remain. **Po Monkey's Lounge** is one of the few. Willie "Po Monkey" Seaberry opened this joint in 1963 and today the joint attracts a diverse crowd including blues fans from around the world and local college students at Delta State University. Visitors are welcome every Thursday night. Po Monkey's is located just north of Cleveland and west of Merigold on Po Monkey Road. Contact Cleveland Tourism at (662) 843-2712 or (800) 295-7473.

McCarty's Pottery is an internationally recognized and award winning pottery business founded by Lee and Pup McCarty in Merigold, just north of Cleveland. The McCarty's began making pottery in 1954 and today their work is featured in museums around the world and sold in many stores. Their pottery includes platters, dishes, lamps, dinnerware, and sculptures. The McCarty's have a store in Merigold where their pottery is for sale while a restaurant and gardens are also part of the store. McCarty's Pottery is located at 101 St. Mary Street in Merigold. Hours: Tue.-Sat. 10-4 P.M. Feb.-Dec. Contact (662) 748-2293.

Another great pottery business in the area is **Peter's Pottery**, which is located north of Cleveland in Mound Bayou. The business began in 1998 by the Woods Brothers (Peter, Joseph, Arthur, and Sandy) and is located at 301 Fortune Avenue in Mound Bayou. Hours: 10-4 P.M. daily (except Wed. & Sun.) Contact (662) 741-2283.

DINING IN CLEVELAND

For dining options in Cleveland, try **Crave Bistro** at 103 South Davis Avenue. Hours: Tue.-Fri. 7-5 P.M., Sat. 9-4 P.M. Contact (662) 843-5222.

INDIANOLA

HISTORY AND ATTRACTIONS

Tracing its history back to the 1880's, Indianola is located at the intersection of Highway 82 and Highway 49 in the heart of the Mississippi Delta region. Indianola has produced several blues musicians and is known as the boyhood home of blues musician B.B. King. **The B.B. King Museum and Delta Interpretive Center** opened in 2008 and showcases the life and career of B.B. King through exhibitions. The museum features a restored brick cotton gin in which King worked in the 1940's, in addition to a large collection of artifacts and memorabilia owned by the musician. The museum also celebrates the rich cultural heritage of the Mississippi Delta region and provides tourist information for Indianola. A yearly **homecoming festival** is held at the museum in honor of B.B. King and features an all-day concert. The museum is located at 400 Second Street in downtown Indianola and admission is required. Hours: Tue.-Sat. 10-5 P.M., Sun.-Mon. 12-5 P.M. (Closed Mondays November to March) Contact (662) 887-9539.

DINING IN INDIANOLA

A trip to Indianola is not complete without lunch at **The Crown Restaurant**. The award-winning restaurant has been featured on several national television stations including the Food Network and magazines such as Southern Living. The restaurant features a full menu of gourmet southern style cooking and also includes a gift shop inside the building. Local art and pottery are displayed on the walls of the restaurant, which has been in business since 1976. The Crown is located at 112 Front Street and is open Tuesday-Friday 9-5 P.M. Contact (662) 887-4522.

The **Indianola Pecan House** is a locally owned business featuring pecan products, pecan pies, candies, and cookies from local sources in a unique gift shop atmosphere. The Indianola Pecan House is located at 1013 Highway 82 East. Hours: Mon.-Fri. 8-5 P.M., Sat. 10-5 P.M. Contact (662) 887-5420 or (800) 541-6252.

LELAND

HISTORY AND ATTRACTIONS

Leland is located on the banks of Deer Creek and historically was a farming town. Located at the intersection of Highway 61 and Highway 82, Leland has produced several blues musicians and is home to the **Highway 61 Blues Museum**. The museum is located inside the old Montgomery Hotel at 307 North Broad Street and features photographs, memorabilia, and information about blues musicians locally and from the Delta region. Admission is required. Hours: Mon.-Sat. 10-5 P.M. Contact (662) 686-7646 or (866) 285-7646.

Leland is also the home of the **Birthplace of Kermit the Frog Museum,** which celebrates the Delta boyhood of Jim Henson, the creator of the "Muppets". The museum features educational exhibits, videos, and memorabilia including Kermit the Frog on display. The museum also has a gift shop and museum staff who can answer questions about Henson and his work. Jim Henson (1936-1990) was born in Greenville and raised in Leland before moving with his family to Maryland in high school. Henson created the Muppets while in college at the University of Maryland and later founded the Jim Henson Company. In the 1970's, Henson helped create characters for Sesame

113

Street and later produced *The Muppet Show*. Henson won two Emmy Awards for his work on *The Storyteller* and *The Jim Henson Hour*. The museum can be found at 415 North Deer Creek Drive and admission is free. Hours: Mon.-Sat. 10-4 P.M. Contact (662) 686-7383.

DINING IN LELAND

For dining options in Leland, try **Lillo's Italian Restaurant,** which has been in business for over 60 years and serves steaks, seafood, pizza, and Italian cuisine. Lillo's is located at Highway 82 and Highway 61. Hours: Tue-Sun. 4:30-9:45 P.M. Contact (662) 686-4401. Also try **Vince's Restaurant** for steaks, seafood, and Italian cuisine at 207 North Main Street. Hours: Thu.-Sun. 5:30-10:45. Contact (662) 686-2112.

GREENVILLE

HISTORY

Founded in 1824, Greenville is located on Lake Ferguson, an oxbow lake of the Mississippi River. Called the "Heart and Soul of the Mississippi Delta Region", Greenville is named after American Revolutionary War hero Nathanael Greene. A 1927 flood caused by a break in the levee of the Mississippi River resulted in catastrophic damage as the city and region was under water for four months. Many of Greenville's historical attractions center around Main Street, Washington Avenue, and Walnut Street. The First National Bank Building, the Washington County Courthouse, and the Hebrew Union Temple can be found in this area. Nationally known retailer Stein Mart was founded in Greenville by Jewish entrepreneurs. Several historic cemeteries are located in Greenville which display the diversity of former residents who helped build the city.

MUSEUMS AND ATTRACTIONS

The **Greenville History Museum** at 409 Washington Avenue has photographs and information about the flood and other important historic events in the city's history. The recently completed Greenville Bridge (2010), a cable-stayed bridge, is the fourth longest such structure in North America and connects Mississippi with Arkansas over the Mississippi River. Hours: Mon.-Fri. 9-5 P.M., Sat. 10-12 P.M. Contact the **Greenville Visitors Bureau** at 216 S. Walnut Street for more information (662) 334-2711 or (800) 467-3582.

The **Winterville Mounds Historic Site** features Indian mounds that predate the Choctaw and Chickasaw Indian tribes (about 1000 to 1450 A.D.). Twelve of the tallest mounds are part of a historic preservation project by the Mississippi Department of Archives and History and the University of Mississippi, including the 55 foot Temple Mound. A National Historic Landmark, the site is located just north of Greenville at 2415 Highway 1. The grounds are open daily and admission is free. The museum hours are: Mon.-Sat. 9-5 P.M. and Sun. 1:30-5 P.M. Contact (662) 334-4684.

The unique **Washington County Welcome Center** is located inside a restored riverboat, which is surrounded by a large pool of water. The "River Road Queen" riverboat was originally built for the 1984 World's Fair in New Orleans. Exhibits on the Delta region and Mississippi can be found inside the riverboat on the first and second floors along with tourist information for the area and region. The center is located at

Highway 82 and Reed Road and is open daily 8-5 P.M. Contact (662) 332-2378.

The **E.E. Bass Cultural Arts Center** is housed inside one of Greenville's most historically significant buildings. The building was designed by renowned architect A. Hays Town and built in 1929. The former school building now hosts community theater performances, art exhibitions, and lectures. The center is located at 323 South Main Street. Hours: Mon.-Fri. 8-4 P.M. Contact (662) 332-2246.

DINING IN GREENVILLE

For dining options in Greenville, **Doe's Eat Place** has received national attention, as the restaurant has been featured on national television networks such as the Food Network and magazines such as Southern Living and Men's Journal. Known for its steaks and tamales, the restaurant has been in business since 1941. Doe's is located at 502 Nelson Street. Hours: Mon.-Sat. 5-9 P.M. Contact (662) 334-3315. Also try **Sherman's Restaurant** at 1400 S. Main Street. Hours: Mon.-Fri. 11-1:30 P.M., 5-9 P.M. Sat. 5-9:30 P.M. Contact (662) 332-6924.

FESTIVALS AND EVENTS

The annual **Delta Blues Festival** in Greenville is the largest blues festival in the Delta region and one of the oldest in the United States. The festival features blues music artists from the region and beyond. The festival began as a community event but has grown larger and into a more professional event today, with food vendors along with live music. The Delta Blues Festival has been a tradition since 1977 and is held in late September. Contact (662) 335-3523.

The annual **Hot Tamale Festival** is held in Greenville, which is known as the Hot Tamale Capital of the World. The festival features the tamale cooking contest, the tamale eating contest, the Miss Hot Tamale contest, the T-shirt and poster contest, and live entertainment. Tamales originate from Latin America and were introduced to the Delta region from Mexican migrant workers after the Great Migration in the early 20th century. Tamales are made of cornmeal, pork or beef, spices, and are wrapped in a corn leaf and cooked by simmering. Several restaurants in Greenville also serve hot tamales. The Hot Tamale Festival is held in October. Contact (662) 378-3121.

The annual **Highway 61 Blues Festival** is held in early October on the banks of the Mississippi River in Warfield Point Park. The festival is part of the **Mighty Mississippi Music Festival** and features live music performances in a variety of genres including blues, rock, country, and heritage. The Delta Village at the festival features food vendors and arts and crafts vendors. Campsite reservations are also available on the river. The festival has been a Greenville tradition since 1999. Contact (662) 347-4223.

GREENWOOD

HISTORY

The first European settlement that later became Greenwood occurred in 1830 on the banks of the Yazoo River. The settlement quickly grew and was incorporated in 1844 as Greenwood, named after Choctaw Chief Greenwood Leflore. Leflore signed the Treaty of Dancing Rabbit Creek, which opened up most of central Mississippi to European settlement. Greenwood grew as a strong cotton market because of its strategic location in the heart of the Delta region. During the Civil War in 1863, General Ulysses Grant's early attempt to siege Vicksburg by way of the Yazoo and Tallahatchie Rivers was stopped near Greenwood by Confederate forces. Grant later chose a different route to siege Vicksburg.

After the war, growth was slow until the addition of railroads in the 1880's, which boosted the cotton industry. Greenwood's Grand Boulevard was once named one of America's ten most beautiful streets by the U.S. Chamber of Commerce and the Garden Clubs of America. The 300 oak trees lining Grand Boulevard were planted in 1916 by Sally Humphreys Guin of the Greenwood Garden Club. In 1950 Guin received recognition for her work by the National Congress of the Daughters of the American Revolution. The Hollywood film *The Help* (2011) was filmed in Greenwood and visitors can tour the locations that were used in the movie, which was based on a novel by Mississippi native Kathryn Stockett.

ATTRACTIONS

Visitor information can be found at the **Greenwood Convention and Visitors Bureau** at 111 East Market Street. Contact (662) 453-9197.

The **Museum of the Mississippi Delta** focuses on the local history, military history, and agricultural history of Greenwood and the region. The museum has a large collection of Native American artifacts including weapons, pottery, and trade beads. Skeletons of Ice Age animals are displayed in the museum and even dinosaur fossils. The museum features photographs and artifacts of the home of Greenwood Leflore, the last Choctaw Tribal Chief before leaving for Oklahoma. A Mississippi art collection is also featured in the museum, which is located at 1608 Highway 82 and a fee is required for admission. The museum also features changing exhibitions on display. Hours: Mon.-Fri. 9-5 P.M., Sat. 10-4 P.M. Contact (662) 453-0925.

Located in Greenwood's historic business district is the **Alluvian Hotel**, a luxury boutique hotel named after the Mississippi alluvial plain. In addition to 45 rooms and five suites, the hotel also features a spa, yoga studio, and an upscale restaurant, **Giardina's**. The Alluvian is located at 318 Howard Street. Contact (662) 451-1500 or (662) 453-2114. The **Leflore County Courthouse** features a beautiful clock tower and Greek columns at Fulton and Market Street. The Yazoo River Bridge connects Grand Boulevard to Fulton Street and Downtown Greenwood.

DINING IN GREENWOOD

Lusco's Restaurant has been in business since 1933 and is one of the oldest and most well-known restaurants in the region and in Mississippi. Lusco's is a family owned restaurant and features steaks, poultry, and seafood. Lusco's is located at 722 Carrollton Avenue. Hours: Tue.-Sat. 5-10 P.M. Contact (662) 453-5365.

FESTIVALS

The **River to the Rails Festival** is the Delta region's premier spring festival and is held in downtown Greenwood in early May. The festival features food vendors, live music, children's activities, a pet parade, a barbeque contest, an art competition, and arts and crafts vendors. Contact (662) 453-7625.

CARROLLTON

HISTORY AND ATTRACTIONS

Carrollton was established in 1834 and was designated as the seat of Carroll County, which was established in 1836. Carrollton is located on Highway 17, which is just north of Highway 82 and 16 miles east of Greenwood. Carrollton is the ancestral home of former U.S. senator J.Z. George, a primary author of the 1890 Mississippi Constitution. Carrollton was also the home of U.S. Senator H.D. Money, author

Elizabeth Spencer, and blues composers Shell Smith and Willie Narmour. Despite a population of only 400, Carrollton has a large historic district, with 18 historic sites around the Courthouse Square. **Carrollton tourist information** can be found at (662) 392-4810.

The **Cotesworth** was the family home of former U.S. Senator J.Z. George. The Cotesworth is a Greek Revival style mansion named after George's friend Cotesworth, who was a Mississippi Supreme Court Chief Justice. The mansion was originally purchased by George in the 1860's and was later expanded. In the 1880's George added a unique hexagonal library near the mansion to house his collection of law books. The mansion stayed in the George family until 2013, when it was sold to the non-profit group Cotesworth Culture and Heritage Center. The mansion was a film location for the movie *The Help*. The Cotesworth is located north of Carrollton on Grenada Road. Contact (662) 392-4810.

The **Merrill Museum** in Carrollton houses the John Sidney McCain collection, which contains personal and military memorabilia of the great grandfather and grandfather of John McCain, U.S. senator and 2008 Presidential candidate. John Sidney McCain and his son both became a U.S. Navy Admiral. The museum is located at 601 E. Jackson Street. Contact (662) 392-4810.

The **Carrollton Historic District** includes historic homes, churches, and buildings which can be visited during a Pilgrimage Tour held in October. Four churches in Carrollton were established in the 1830's and all have active congregations. Tours of the Carrollton historic district are available. Contact (662) 392-4810.

BELZONI

HISTORY

Located on the Yazoo River in Humphreys County and the Mississippi Delta region, Belzoni was first settled by Europeans in the late 1800's and was founded in 1895. Belzoni was named for 19th century Italian archaeologist and explorer Giovanni Battista Belzoni. Belzoni has been called the Farm-Raised Catfish Capital of the World since it produces more farm-raised catfish than any other county in the United States (even though several other towns also claim this title). **Belzoni tourist information** can be found at 111 Magnolia Street. Contact (662) 247-4838 or (800) 408-4838.

FESTIVALS AND ATTRACTIONS

The **World Catfish Festival** is held every April in Belzoni and has been named a Top 100 event in North America and a Top 20 event in the southeast. The festival began in 1976 and today attracts thousands of visitors to downtown Belzoni. The festival features arts and crafts vendors, live entertainment, children's activities, a 5K run, and the crowning of Miss Catfish and Little Miss Catfish pageants.

There are 42 beautifully painted **catfish sculptures** at various locations throughout Belzoni that are displayed permanently. Each standing five feet tall, the custom mold sculptures were designed by a Chicago company and painted by volunteers in the community. The **Catfish Museum and Welcome Center** is located at 111 Magnolia Street in downtown Belzoni. The museum displays the rich history of Belzoni

121

including handmade crafts and video presentations of the catfish tradition. Hours: Mon.-Fri. 9-5 P.M. Contact (662) 247-4838 or (800) 408-4838.

The **Jaketown Site** is an ancient Native American village which is located north of Belzoni on Highway 7. Archaeologists believe the village site was inhabited as early as 1750 B.C. Evidence shows that the inhabitants lived in small huts and used tools, projectiles, beads, gorgets (pendants), effigies (sculptures), and items from stone which must have been brought from great distances. The inhabitants are believed to be among the first in the Lower Mississippi Valley to have a civilized culture. The **Jaketown Museum** at 116 West Jackson Street in Belzoni showcases information and artifacts found at the site, which was declared a National Historic Landmark in 1990. Admission is free. Hours: Mon.-Fri. 10-4 P.M. Contact (662) 247-2151.

Wister Gardens was developed by Frances Chiles Henry and Wister Henry in 1937. Known as the Delta's Garden, the beautiful gardens feature 14 acres of azaleas, roses, daylilies, and crape myrtles along trails and drives while a variety of ducks and swans can be seen on the lake. A gazebo inside the gardens frequently hosts outdoor weddings and a large fountain from Italy installed over a well contains large goldfish and water lilies. A garden house on the property is available for reservation. The gardens offer free admission and are located just north of Belzoni on Highway 7. Contact (662) 836-6471.

On display at the **Ethel Wright Mohamed Stitchery Museum** is a collection of artwork painted on fabric which represents the stories of the family life of Ethel Wright Mohamed, including her marriage and eight children. The artwork also represents life in the Mississippi Delta region and has been recognized by the Smithsonian Institute. The museum can be found at 307 Central Street and a small admission fee is required. Hours: Mon.-Fri. 9-5 P.M. Contact (662) 247-1433.

The ancient cypress trees of **Sky Lake** are some of the largest and oldest trees in North America and are one of the last remaining tracts of old growth cypress trees on Earth. The baldcypress or cypress tree is classified in the Cupressaceae family, the same family as the famous giant sequoia and redwood trees of California. These trees, a wetlands species, grow very large trunks and produce small cones and needlelike foliage. Cypress trees reproduce and thrive in very wet conditions where other trees cannot. Cypress trees can grow in other soil types but by growing where there is less competition, they can become giants. Some of the cypress trees here at Sky Lake could be as old as 2,000 years. **The Sky Lake boardwalk** was opened in 2011 and is located 7 miles north of Belzoni. The 12 foot tall boardwalk allows visitors to see the ancient cypress trees for over 1,700 feet through the forest canopy. Contact the Sky Lake Wildlife Management Association at (662) 453-5409.

DINING IN BELZONI

For dining options in Belzoni, try the **Lunch Basket Express** at 16814 Highway 49, which features Southern cuisine. Contact (662) 247-9930.

YAZOO CITY

HISTORY

Yazoo City is located on the banks of the Yazoo River and lies on the edge of the hills and the Mississippi River alluvial plain known as the Delta Region. The Yazoo River was named by French explorer Robert LaSalle in 1682 after the Yazoo Indians living near the mouth of the river. Yazoo County was created in 1823 when the land was opened up to settlement after the Treaty of Doak's Stand in 1820. Planning of a port city began by landowners in 1828 at the future site of Yazoo City and the town was named Manchester. Lots were sold beginning in 1830. By 1834, all lots were sold and construction of businesses and homes began. Steamboats regularly passed through the port and in 1841 citizens voted to change the name of the city to Yazoo City in honor of the river that drove the local economy. Yazoo City became the county seat in 1848 and a stately new courthouse was constructed.

Several epidemics of yellow fever swept through Yazoo City in the 1850's and particularly in 1853 when many citizens perished. During the Vicksburg Campaign of the Civil War, Yazoo City was temporarily occupied by Union forces and invaded six times. The last invasion was the worst, causing major destruction and the burning of the courthouse. A historical marker commemorates the **Battle of Benton Road** at Highway 49 and Broadway Hill. In 1864, Union forces defended Yazoo City against Confederate forces led by Generals Lawrence Ross and Robert Richardson.

The 1870's was a time of rebuilding and growth for Yazoo City with the cotton industry. The railroad was built in 1884, electricity came in 1888, and streetlights were installed. By 1900, Yazoo City had close to 5,000 residents. A great catastrophe happened in 1904 when a fire broke out and destroyed the downtown business district, more than 100 homes, and many churches. A few buildings survived including the 1872 courthouse, the new library, and several antebellum homes. No lives were lost in the fire and the town was rebuilt. Today, Main Street is lined with brightly painted brick buildings housing stores and businesses which were built after the fire. Yazoo City is the hometown of former Governor Haley Barbour and comedian Jerry Clower was a longtime resident.

ATTRACTIONS AND EVENTS

Tourist information for Yazoo City can be found at 110 Jerry Clower Boulevard. Contact (662) 746-1815 or (800) 381-0662. Yazoo City is located on Highway 49 and is 45 miles northwest of Jackson.

Ricks Memorial Library is the oldest public library in Mississippi still in use and is located at 310 North Main Street. Built in 1900, the library is a Mississippi Literary Landmark because of its association with author Willie Morris. The library is open daily except Sunday. Contact (662) 746-5557.

Glenwood Cemetery is one of Yazoo City's most unique attractions. Originating from 1856, the cemetery holds a mass grave of unknown Confederate soldiers. The most notable section of the cemetery is the "Witches Grave," which is surrounded by chains and according to legend holds the Witch of Yazoo, who broke out of the chains and burned down the city in 1904. The legend became famous from the book written by author Willie Morris *"Good Ole Boy"*. Tours of the cemetery are available by appointment. Contact (662) 746-1815 or (800) 381-0662.

The **Jerry Clower Festival** is held on historic Main Street in Yazoo City in early May in honor of comedian and former resident Jerry Clower. The festival features food vendors, arts and crafts, live music, and family fun. The free festival also hosts a 5K run, a parade of cars, and an antique and classic car show. Contact (662) 746-7676.

DINING IN YAZOO CITY

For dining options in Yazoo City, try **Ubon's Restaurant** for great barbeque, burgers, and southern cooking at 801 Jerry Clower Boulevard. Hours: 10 A.M.-11 P.M. daily. Contact (662) 716-7100.

THE HILLS REGION OF NORTH MISSISSIPPI

The Hills of North Mississippi region contains the cities of Southaven, Olive Branch, Horn Lake, and Hernando. These cities are part of Desoto County, which is just south of Memphis. The region also contains the historical town of Holly Springs, the historical college town of Oxford, and the birthplace and boyhood home of Elvis Presley in Tupelo. The region also contains the historical Civil War battlefields of Baldwyn, Corinth, and Iuka. Tishomingo County contains some of the most beautiful natural areas in the state and the Natchez Trace Parkway provides a scenic drive. Several major lakes are also included in the region which feature camping and recreational facilities.

SOUTHAVEN

ATTRACTIONS

Southaven is the largest city in Desoto County and shares a border with the state of Mississippi and Tennessee. Incorporated in 1981, Southaven is also the third largest city in Mississippi at just over 50,000 residents. The rapid growth of Southaven is attributed to residents of Memphis and other areas seeking a higher quality of life. Southaven is located south of

Memphis on Interstate 55. Southaven tourist information can be found at 4716 Pepper Chase Drive in Southaven. Contact (662) 393-8770.

Snowden Grove Amphitheater hosts nationally known performers in a variety of music genres in an outdoor setting. The amphitheater features chair-back seating and a grass lawn. Opened in 2006, the amphitheater is one of the top entertainment venues in the region and has hosted top performers of country music, rock, hip-hop, and more. Snowden Grove can be found at 6285 Snowden Lane. Contact (662) 892-2660.

The **Landers Center** is a large indoor arena which hosts a variety of sports and entertainment events. Professional hockey, a variety of music concerts, and rodeos are some of the events hosted at the center along with a convention center and theater. The Landers Center can be found near the intersection of Interstate 55 and Church Road. Contact (662) 280-9120 or (888) 280-9120.

Southaven Towne Center is an upscale shopping center featuring major nationally known stores and is located at Interstate 55 and Goodman Road. Hours: Mon.-Sat. 10 A.M.-9 P.M., Sun. 12-6 P.M. Contact (731) 668-7621.

FESTIVALS AND EVENTS

The annual **Crystal Ball** is a large charity event which benefits the Community Foundation of Northwest Mississippi and attracts visitors from across Mississippi and the surrounding states. During the ball, performances are held to entertain the guests and a different theme is chosen each year. The event is held at the Arena at Southaven on January 1st and has been a tradition since 2000. Contact (662) 449-5002.

The annual **Mid-South Fair** is a 10 day event held in mid-September at the Landers Center. The fair features a variety of attractions including amusement rides, live entertainment, livestock and beauty contests. The fair has been a tradition since 1856 and was held in Memphis for many years before being relocated to Southaven. Contact (901) 274-8800.

DINING IN SOUTHAVEN

For dining options in Southaven, try **Maria's Cantina** for great Mexican cuisine at 6717 Airways Boulevard. Hours: Mon.-Thu. 11-8:30 P.M., Fri.-Sat. 11 A.M.-12 A.M., Sun. 11-9 P.M. Contact (662) 772-5926.

OLIVE BRANCH

HISTORY AND ATTRACTIONS

Incorporated in 1875, Olive Branch is also a rapid growing city which borders Southaven to the east. Similar to Southaven, Olive Branch is attracting many new residents from Memphis and other areas because of a high quality of life. **Old Towne Olive Branch** is a historic business district that dates back to the 1930's and features locally owned shops and eateries. Old Towne is located at the intersection of Goodman Road and Pidgeon Roost Road. Contact (662) 393-8770 for tourist information.

Brussel's Bonsai Nursery offers the largest selection of indoor and outdoor bonsai trees for sale in the United States. The nursery is housed in a 175,000 square foot greenhouse facility and caters to gardeners and Asian culture enthusiasts. Bonsai is a Japanese art form that focuses on miniature trees grown in containers or pots. The nursery is located at 8125 Center Hill Road in Olive Branch. Hours: Mon.-Fri. 8 A.M.-4:30 P.M. Contact (800) 582-2593.

DINING IN OLIVE BRANCH

For dining options in Olive Branch, try **Sweet Pea's Table** at 8948 Midsouth Drive. Hours: Tue.-Thu. 11-8 P.M., Fri.-Sat. 11-9 P.M., Sun. 11-2 P.M. Contact (662) 895-7743.

HORN LAKE

HISTORY AND ATTRACTIONS

The City of Horn Lake was officially incorporated in 1973, although its history dates back to the early 1800's. Bordering Southaven to the west, Horn Lake received its name from an oxbow lake lying three miles to the west that was a former channel of the Mississippi River. The river changed course in the late 18th century, leaving a body of water resembling a cow horn. The Chickasaw Indians originally inhabited the area but relinquished all claims to the land in 1832 with the Treaty of Pontotoc. European settlement began soon afterward. Cotton and railroads grew the local economy.

Two known **antebellum homes** exist today in Horn Lake and these are privately owned residences. "**Mon Amour**" is a two story octagonal-shaped home built in 1844 by Dr. Nathaniel Raines and is one of only two known antebellum octagonal-shaped homes in Mississippi (the other being Longwood in Natchez). The home has been restored by Mr. Brian Swilly. The **Walker Home** is a four room log home built in the middle 1800's. Contact the City of Horn Lake for more information about the homes at (662) 393-6178.

An exciting tourist development for Horn Lake and the region is the recent purchase of the Circle G Ranch, which was once owned by Elvis

129

and Priscilla Presley. The owners plan to renovate the ranch into a tourist attraction including the honeymoon cottage of Elvis and Priscilla. Contact the **Horn Lake Chamber of Commerce** at (662) 393-9897 for more information.

Horn Lake is also home to the **American Contract Bridge League Museum**, which contains the world's largest collection of bridge memorabilia. The state of the art interactive museum contains trophies, videos, and other artifacts and exhibits focused on the game of bridge. The museum also contains the American Contract Bridge League Hall of Fame and a library. The museum is located at 6575 Windchase Boulevard and admission is free. Hours: Mon.-Fri. 8-4:45 P.M. Contact (662) 253-3100.

DINING IN HORN LAKE

For dining options in Horn Lake, try **Memphis Barbeque Company** at 709 Desoto Cove. Hours: Sun.-Thur. 11-10 P.M., Fri.-Sat. 11-11 P.M. Contact (662) 536-3763.

HERNANDO

HISTORY AND ATTRACTIONS

Named after Hernando De Soto, Hernando is the county seat of Desoto County and is the location of the courthouse in the historic town square on Highway 51 and Commerce Street. Hernando was incorporated in 1840, four years after the formation of Desoto County in 1836. **Commerce Street** has a variety of locally owned shops featuring antiques, art, pottery, and jewelry. The **Desoto County Museum** is located at 111 East Commerce Street and provides historical information about the county. Exhibits include local Native American history, Civil War battles that affected Desoto County, local celebrities such as John Grisham, Jerry Lee Lewis, and a restored log cabin. Hours: Tue.-Sat. 10-5 P.M. Admission is free. Contact (662) 429-8852.

The **Desoto County Welcome Center** offers tourist information about Desoto County and the state of Mississippi and is located at Interstate 55, Church Road, and Pepper Chase Drive. **Arkabutla Lake** is located near Hernando and offers boating, fishing, hiking trails, campgrounds and a swimming beach. The lake is known for bass, catfish, and crappie. The lake can be located from Highway 51 and Arkabutla Road. The lake has a visitor center with information about campgrounds and maps. Contact (662) 562-6261.

For dining options in Hernando, try **Windy City Grille** at 330 West Commerce Street. Hours: Sun.-Thu.11-10:15 P.M., Fri.-Sat. 11-11 P.M. Contact (662) 449-0331.

HOLLY SPRINGS

HISTORY AND ATTRACTIONS

Holly Springs was incorporated in 1837 and named county seat of the newly formed Marshall County. Chickasaw Indians originally inhabited the area until the early 1830's. By 1855, a railroad was constructed through Holly Springs and by the end of the century the railroad was connected to larger cities. During the Civil War, Holly Springs was used

131

by General Ulysses S. Grant as a supply depot and headquarters, which was demolished in 1862 in a raid by Confederate General Earl Van Dorn and his forces. In 1878, the yellow fever epidemic took the lives of 2,000 residents of Holly Springs and the Marshall County Courthouse was used as a hospital during the epidemic.

The **Holly Springs Tourism Bureau** is located at 148 College Street and can provide tourist information, maps, and brochures. Contact (662) 252-2515 or (888) 687-4765.

Rust College was established in 1866 by the Freedman's Aid Society of the Methodist Episcopal Church. After having several different names, the school name was eventually changed to Rust College by 1915. Rust College is one of the oldest historically black colleges in the United States and the oldest associated with the United Methodist Church. Rust College is located at North Memphis Street. Contact (662) 252-2491 for more information. **Court Square Inn** at 132 East College Avenue is a historic bed and breakfast with three luxury suites inside a recently renovated (1865) building on courthouse square. Contact (800) 926-3686.

Holly Springs has over 25 antebellum homes and buildings and many are available for tours. The annual **Holly Springs Pilgrimage** is held in April and features a tour of historic antebellum homes, churches, cemeteries, and other historic sites. Tours are given by costumed guides and include horse-drawn carriage rides, Civil War re-enactors, luncheons, and a dinner. The Pilgrimage has been a tradition since 1938 and is sponsored by the Holly Springs Garden Club. Contact the **Holly Springs Tourism Bureau** for tour information (888) 687-4765.

The **Marshall County Historical Museum** has one of the largest collections of Civil War memorabilia in Mississippi, including over 40,000 artifacts inside a three story building. Many of the items are associated with the role of Holly Springs in the Civil War. The museum is located at 220 East College Avenue. Hours: Mon.-Fri. 10-4 P.M. Contact (662) 252-3669.

The **Walter Place** is one of the most impressive mansions in the southeast. The Greek Revival and Gothic Revival style mansion was built in 1860 by wealthy lawyer and railroad builder Harvey Washington Walker. Walker wanted the mansion to be the finest in Holly Springs. During the Civil War, General Ulysses S. Grant's wife Julia stayed in the mansion with their son and slave until the night before the Van Dorn raid. The estate includes two English basement cottages and a 15 acre botanical garden with walking trails and a natural waterfall among the trees and seasonal flowers. The mansion is located at 300 West Chulahoma Avenue. Contact (662) 252-2515.

Montrose Mansion was built by Alfred Brooks as a wedding gift to his daughter Margaret, who died shortly after the birth of her fifth child. This Greek Revival home was built in 1858 and was later given to Holly Springs by a will after Margaret's death. The will stated that the mansion must be rented to the Holly Springs Garden Club for one dollar a month for 100 years. Montrose was also featured in several movies, including *Heart of Dixie* and *Third of July, 1862*. The interior includes a beautiful circular staircase, parquet floors, cornices, and ceiling medallions. Surrounding Montrose is an arboretum that contains 50 species of native trees. Montrose is the home of the Holly Springs Garden Club, who sponsors the Holly Springs Pilgrimage. Montrose is located at 335 Salem Avenue. Contact (662) 252-2515 for tour information.

The **Burton Place** was built by Mary Malvina Shields Burton in 1848 using the Federal style. An Italian portico (porch) was added later to the mansion and the cast iron fence surrounding the mansion once surrounded the courthouse. Burton and her husband frequently travelled the world and were friends with Sam Houston, whom they frequently invited to their mansion. The walls of Burton Place are over two feet thick, each window has two sets of frames, and each doorway has two doors. The mansion contains many original furnishings and is located at 248 South Memphis Street. Contact (662) 252-2515 for tour information.

Airliewood is a Gothic Revival style home built for planter Will Henry Coxe in 1858. General Ulysses S. Grant occupied the home as his military headquarters during the Civil War while Union soldiers camped on the grounds. The **Magnolias** is a Gothic Revival style home built in 1852 by William F. Mason for his daughter as a wedding gift. The home was used in the movie *Cookies Fortune* in 1999. **Athenia** was built in 1858 by Judge J.W. Clapp, who was a member of the Confederate Congress. The Greek Revival style home was later owned by General Absolom M. West, who was nominated to be Vice President twice. Contact (662) 252-2515 for tour information about these homes.

Historical churches in Holly Springs include **Christ Episcopal Church** (1858), which features an octagonal spire, 16 stained glass windows, and a Pilcher pipe organ at 100 North Randolph Street. The church was used as a stable for horses for Union forces during the Civil War. Contact (662) 252-2584. **First United Methodist Church** (1849) features circular twin staircases and a Pilcher organ at 175 East Van Dorn Avenue. Contact (662) 252-1439. **First Presbyterian Church** (1860) was completed at 164 South Memphis Street after all construction stopped during the Civil War. The lower level served as a stable for horses of the Union forces while ammunition was stored in the upper level of the church. Contact (662) 252-4678. The **Church of the Yellow Fever Martyrs** was built in 1841 by the Episcopalian Church but was later sold to the Catholic Church. The church was completely disassembled and moved to its current location at 305 East College Avenue. Church members cared for yellow fever victims here and eventually died themselves from the fever. Contact (662) 252-7552.

OUTDOOR ATTRACTIONS

A top destination for nature lovers in Mississippi, **Strawberry Plains Audubon Center** is a large natural outdoor area that includes an antebellum home. Ruth Finley and Margaret Finley Shackelford entrusted their home and property to the National Audubon Society, who has a mission of restoring and conserving 3,000 acres of hardwood forests, wetlands, and grasslands at Strawberry Plains. Included at the property is a visitor center, the antebellum Davis home, 15 miles of hiking trails, native gardens and wildflowers, restored forest and grasslands, ponds, a plant nursery, and wildlife viewing areas. The home was built by Ebenezer Davis in 1851 and was routinely attacked by Union forces in the Civil War. The home was the only one in Holly Springs to be burned during the war. The family lived in the remains of the partially burned home until the 1970's when it was renovated by a family relative. Tours of the Davis home are available by appointment only. The Audubon Center requires admission and can be found at 285 Plains Road. Hours: Tue.-Sat. 8-4 P.M. Contact (662) 252-1155 for tours.

DINING IN HOLLY SPRINGS

A stop in Holly Springs is not complete without a burger from **Phillip's Grocery**. Located at 541 East Van Dorn Avenue, the establishment originally was a saloon in 1892 and became a grocery store in 1919. Mr. and Mrs. Phillips bought the place in 1948 and began grilling hamburgers. Phillips Grocery has been recognized by national publications such as USA Today, Gourmet Magazine, Men's Journal, L.A. Times, and Mississippi Magazine. The restaurant inside feels like a step back in time with nostalgic memorabilia on the walls of the century-old building. In addition to burgers, Phillips grocery also serves breakfast food, deli sandwiches, salads, and deserts. Hours: Mon.-Fri. 10-4 P.M., Sat. 10-6 P.M. Contact (662) 252-4671.

Even with the many antebellum homes in Holly Springs, many say the top attraction in Holly Springs is **Graceland Too**, a two-story home owned by die-hard Elvis fan Paul McLeod. McLeod has over the years collected a large variety of Elvis Presley memorabilia and displayed them inside his home, including Elvis posters, photographs, stamps, and Elvis candy wrappers. The museum was open 24 hours a day and was once painted pink, white, and more recently blue. In July 2014, McLeod passed away and the status of the museum is unclear. Contact the Holly Springs Tourism Bureau for more information (662) 252-2515. The museum is located at 200 East Gholson Avenue.

OXFORD

HISTORY

Oxford was incorporated in 1837 and was built on land that once was inhabited by the Chickasaw Indians. Lafayette County had been established a year earlier and named for Marquis de Lafayette, a young French aristocrat who fought alongside the Americans in the Revolutionary War. The Mississippi Legislature voted in 1841 to make Oxford the home of the first state university, the University of Mississippi. The town was named Oxford (after Oxford, England) in hopes of being selected as the location of the university. The University of Mississippi opened in 1848 to 80 students and has grown ever since. During the Civil War in 1864, Oxford was severely devastated when Union forces burned many buildings in town, including the Courthouse and surrounding buildings on the town square. Oxford residents and students were killed during the war.

During the Civil Rights Movement of the 1960's, turmoil arose when James Meredith enrolled in the university as the first African American student. Violent riots and protests occurred on campus including two deaths. Eventually race relations improved on campus, however. Today, 13 percent of the enrollment at the university is African American and Meredith has a statue on campus. Oxford is known as the home of Nobel Prize winning author William Faulkner and is known as a literary destination by several national magazines.

ATTRACTIONS

The historic town square has always been the center of business and culture in Oxford. The historic downtown square or **"the Square"** is known as the section of downtown Oxford home to a variety of boutique shops, bookstores, art galleries, and restaurants along with the courthouse square. The Square has been the center of business and culture in Oxford since 1837. **Square Books** is an iconic independent bookstore located at 160 Courthouse Square. Hours: Mon-Thu. 9 A.M.-9 P.M., Fri.-Sat. 9-10 P.M., Sunday until 9-6 P.M. Contact (662) 236-2262. **Nielson's Department Store** was established in 1839 and is the oldest department store in the South, featuring men's and women's clothing at 119 Courthouse Square. Hours: Mon.-Sat. 9-5:30 P.M. Contact (662) 234-1161. The Square has been featured in national magazines and is also the center of nightlife in Oxford. Visitors can find information, maps, and brochures at the **Oxford Visitors Center**, which is located at 415 South Lamar Boulevard. Contact (662) 232-2477.

The home of **William Faulkner** is arguably the top attraction in Oxford. Born in 1897, William Faulkner grew up in Oxford with his family and spent most of his life here. Faulkner won the Nobel Prize for Literature in 1949 and the Pulitzer Prize for Fiction in 1955 and 1963. **Rowan Oak** was built in 1844 and became the home of Faulkner in 1930 until his death in 1962. Visitors can tour the home where Faulkner produced his famous literary works, including an outline of his famous novel *A Fable*. The home is located on Old Taylor Road and admission is charged. The Greek Revival style home was declared a National Historic Landmark in 1968. Hours: Tue.-Sat. 10-4 P.M., Sun. 1-4 P.M. Contact (662) 234-3284.

Cedar Oaks is a Greek Revival style home built in 1859 by William Turner. The home was set on fire in 1864 during the Civil War by Union forces but survived the fire as Molly Turner Orr gathered a fire brigade to save the home. A century later the home was moved about two miles from its original location in 1963 to avoid expanding business in the city. Cedar Oaks is known locally as "the house that would not die" and is located at 601 Murray Drive. Contact (662) 232-2367 for tour information.

St. Peter's Cemetery is the burial place of many of Oxford's citizens, including William Faulkner and L.Q.C. Lamar. The cemetery is located a few blocks north of the Square inside a residential neighborhood (Jefferson Avenue and 16th Street). Contact (662) 232-2477 or (800) 758-9177.

CAMPUS ATTRACTIONS

The **University of Mississippi** is commonly referred to as "Ole Miss" and has several historical attractions on campus. **The Lyceum** is the oldest building on campus. Completed in 1848, the Lyceum was the only survivor of the five original buildings at the university after the Civil War. With Greek Revival style architecture, the building is a landmark on campus at University Circle. Contact (662) 915-7211 for more information.

The **Center for the Study of Southern Culture** is located inside Barnard Observatory on campus and serves a unique purpose. The center focuses on regional studies and has produced the Encyclopedia of Southern Culture, Living Blues Magazine, and co-hosts the annual Faulkner Conference. The center features changing photographic exhibits throughout the year and is located at Grove Loop on campus. Hours: Mon.-Fri. 8-5 P.M. Contact (662) 915-5993 for more information.

The **Gertrude Ford Center for Performing Arts** is a state of the art facility completed in 2002. The 88,000 square foot facility hosts a variety of performing arts events and hosted a 2008 Presidential debate between then senators Barack Obama and John McCain. The center is located at 100 University Avenue. Contact (662) 915-2787 for more information.

The **University of Mississippi Museum** is a series of buildings on campus featuring Southern Folk Art, Greek and Roman Antiques, 19th century scientific instruments, American fine art, and changing exhibitions. The museum can be found at University Avenue and Fifth Street and admission is free for the permanent collection. Hours: Tue.-Sat. 10-6 P.M. Contact (662) 915-7073.

The **Burns Belfry Museum and Multicultural Center** features exhibits focused on African-American history from slavery to civil rights. Also featured is the history of the old Burns Church, which was organized by freed slaves in 1869 and was the first African-American church in Oxford. The current church building was built in 1910 and was influential to the lives of many African-Americans until 1974, when the congregation moved to a new location. The historic church building went through several owners until the last owner, John Grisham, donated the building to the Oxford-Lafayette County Heritage Foundation. The church was renovated in 2013 by the Heritage Foundation and the Oxford Development Association with the help of federal, state, and local grants. The historic church building is now a museum and is located at 710 Jackson Avenue. Hours: Wed.-Fri. 12-3 P.M., Sun. 1-4 P.M. Contact (662) 281-9963.

DINING IN OXFORD

Ajax Diner is located at 118 Courthouse Square and focuses on Southern cooking and cocktails, plate lunches, sandwiches and po-boys, salads and steaks for dinner. This award-winning restaurant is owned by John Currence and is open Monday-Saturday 11:30-10 P.M. Contact (662) 232-8880.

City Grocery is located at 152 Courthouse Square and has specialized in fine Southern dining by Chef John Currence since 1992. This award winning restaurant is located inside a historic two-story building. Hours: Mon.-Wed. 11:30-2:30 P.M., 6-10 P.M. Thu.-Sat. 11:30-2:30, 6-10:30 P.M. Contact (662) 232-8080.

FESTIVALS AND EVENTS

The **Oxford Film Festival** is an annual four day event which celebrates independent films of varying genres and film producers from around the world. The nationally-recognized festival was created in 2003 and is held in early February at the Oxford Malco Commons cinema. Contact (877) 560-3456.

The annual **Double Decker Arts Festival** in Oxford is a two-day family event which features live music, food vendors, arts and crafts. The festival has been a tradition since 1996 and is held in late April at the historic Courthouse Square. The festival is also known for the two-floor red buses which transport visitors. Contact (662) 232-2367.

SARDIS, ENID, AND GRENADA

Three major lakes are found in North-central Mississippi and each features a state park. **Sardis Lake** is a 58,500 acre lake located near Oxford and can be accessed by way of Highway 314 from Oxford or by way of Interstate 55 and Highway 315. Contact (662) 563-4531 for more information. The Highway 315 entrance gives access to **John W. Kile State Park,** which is located on the shores of Sardis Lake. Highway 35 by way of Interstate 55 also gives access to the park. The park attractions include 200 developed campsites, 20 air conditioned cabins, boating, fishing, golf, jet skiing, a visitor center lodge, and parking. Reservations are recommended for campsites and cabins. Sardis Lake is known for catfish, crappie, bass, and bream. The main park is located from Highway 315 while the campgrounds are located on the lower lake from Highway 35. Contact (662) 487-1345 for more information.

Enid Lake is a 44,000 acre lake located about 26 miles south of Sardis Lake and can be accessed from Interstate 55 and Highway 32. Contact (662) 563-4571 for more information. **George Payne Cossar State Park** is located on the shores of Enid Lake. Enid Lake is a top fishing destination, as the world record crappie was pulled from this lake. In addition to fishing, the lake and park offers 76 developed campgrounds (including RV), 13 air conditioned cabins, boating, water skiing, visitor center, and nature trails. Contact (662) 623-7356 for more information.

Grenada Lake is a 64,000 acre lake located 20 miles south of Enid Lake and can be accessed from Interstate 55 and Highway 8. Contact (662) 226-5911 for more information. Tourist information can also be found at the **Grenada Tourism Commission** at 95 S.W. Frontage Road. Contact (662) 226-2060 or (800) 373-2571. **Hugh White State Park** is located on the shores of Grenada Lake from Highway 8. The park offers 158 developed campsites (including RV), 25 air conditioned cabins, golf, fishing, boating, water skiing, visitor center, and nature trails. Grenada Lake is known for its great fishing, in particular crappie but also bass, bream, and catfish. Dogwoods golf course at the park has been ranked in the top 10 courses in Mississippi. Contact (662) 226-4934 for more information.

DINING IN GRENADA

For dining options near Grenada, try **333 Restaurant** at the main entrance to Grenada Lake (515 Scenic Loop 333) for steaks, seafood, southern buffet, burgers and sandwiches. Hours: Mon.-Wed. 11-3 P.M.,

Thu.11-9 P.M., Fri.-Sat.11-10 P.M., Sun. 11-3 P.M. Contact (662) 229-0020.

FESTIVALS AND EVENTS

The **Thunder on the Water Festival** is a four day event featuring amusement rides, food vendors, arts and crafts, an auto show, a 5K run, fishing tournaments, live music and entertainment. The festival is held at Grenada Lake in June. Contact (662) 226-2060.

Balloons Over Grenada is a two-day festival which features hot air balloons glowing at night, a balloon race in the morning, live music, a carnival, balloon rides, and children's activities. The festival is held in August at Grenada Lake. Contact (662) 226-2060.

TUPELO

HISTORY

Tupelo was incorporated as a city in 1870 and named after the Tupelo gum tree. The Tupelo area was originally inhabited by the Chickasaw Indians. Hernando De Soto is known to have passed through the area in 1540 before discovering the Mississippi River. In 1736 during the French and Indian War, a bloody battle was fought near Tupelo between the British-armed Chickasaw Indians and the invading forces of the French and the Choctaw Indians. Known as the **Battle of Ackia**, the battle left the area in strong British control and contributed to the eventual domination of North America by the British. The **Natchez Trace Parkway** was established by the Chickasaw Indians as a commerce route to the Natchez Indian territory to the southwest. The British used the route in the 18th century. During the Civil War of the

1860's, Union and Confederate forces collided in the **Battle of Tupelo** in 1864. The result of this battle ensured the safety of Union General William T. Sherman's supply lines. Tupelo was at the intersection of two major railroads built in 1887 and this contributed greatly to the growth of the town. Today, Tupelo is a major center of business, industry, and healthcare in addition to being the birthplace of Elvis Presley.

ATTRACTIONS

The **Tupelo Convention and Visitors Bureau** can provide information about attractions in town including maps and brochures and is located at 399 East Main Street. Contact (662) 841-6521 or (800) 533-0611.

The birth place of **Elvis Presley** is the top attraction in Tupelo as many fans of Elvis come here to visit his boyhood home and the town in which he grew up. Located on the Elvis birthplace site is the two room house in which he was born, a museum containing Elvis memorabilia, and the childhood church building of Elvis Presley. The house, museum, and church can be toured for a fee. Also located on the grounds of the birthplace is a statue of Elvis at age 13 along with various music trail markers for blues and country music, a memorial chapel, a story wall, fountain of life, car exhibit, and a gift shop. The Elvis Birthplace and Museum is located at 306 Elvis Presley Drive (off Main Street). Hours: Mon.-Sat. 9-5:30 P.M., Sun. 1-5 P.M. Contact (662) 841-1245 for more information.

A driving tour of Tupelo sites which were significant in the childhood of Elvis can also be arranged. These sites include the Lee County Courthouse, the Milam Elementary School, and the Tupelo Hardware Company. The **Tupelo Auto Museum** features in its collection a car that Elvis gave away and a collection of Elvis posters. The **Tupelo Elvis Festival** is also held the first weekend in June and features music, food,

143

and activities in downtown. The birthplace site is located at 306 Elvis Presley Drive by way of Main Street. **Tupelo Hardware Company** was founded in 1925 by the same family as the current owners. In January 1945, 10-year old Elvis received a guitar purchased by his mother Gladys Presley at this store, which is located at 114 West Main Street. Hours: Mon.-Fri. 7-5:30 P.M., Sat. 7-12 P.M., Contact (662) 842-4637.

Tupelo National Battlefield is administered by the National Park Service. This is the site of the July 1864 battle between Union and Confederate forces in which neither side had a clear victory but Union forces succeeded in their main goal of keeping Confederate forces away from Union railroads in Tennessee. Today, the battlefield is a one acre monument located on Main Street (Highway 6) at the intersection with Monument Drive. Contact (662) 680-4025 or (800) 305-7417.

The **Natchez Trace Parkway** extends 444 miles from Natchez, Mississippi to Nashville, Tennessee. The parkway originated 8,000 years ago as dirt paths through the forest created by travelers (including Native Americans and Europeans) and their wild animals. Today the parkway is a scenic two lane highway free of commercial development with many exits and stops for the convenience of travelers. The parkway is popular not only with motorists but also with bikers, runners, and hikers. Headquartered in Tupelo, the Parkway is maintained and administered by the U.S. Department of the Interior. At the **parkway headquarters** is a visitor center located at milepost 266 which features a variety of exhibits, displays, maps, and information. Hours: 8-5 P.M. daily. Contact (662) 680-4025 or (800) 305-7417.

The **Tupelo Auto Museum** features a collection of more than 100 vintage cars valued at over $6 million and is displayed inside a modern 120,000 square foot facility. Exhibits include a 19th century steam-powered vehicle, an 1886 Benz, a Duesenberg, a DeLorean and a rare Tucker. Also on display is the 1976 Lincoln purchased by **Elvis Presley** and given as a gift. The museum is located at 1 Otis Boulevard just off

Main Street and Highway 45 and admission is required. Hours: Mon.-Sat. 9-4:30 P.M., Sun. 12-4:30 P.M. Contact (662) 842-4242.

Adjacent to the auto museum is the **Bancorp South Arena**, a modern arena which hosts a variety of music concerts, ice skating, trade shows, basketball, and hockey. The arena is located at 375 East Main Street. Contact (662) 841-6528.

The **Tupelo Buffalo Park** originally began with a few buffalo on a cattle farm. Today a herd of buffalo and over 300 exotic animals can be found on a 200 acre park, which attracts over 100,000 visitors per year. Some of the animals include lions, tigers, cougars, bears, camels, exotic birds, giraffes, kangaroos, snakes, and zebras. Visitors ride in the monster bison bus (a converted school bus) to see the bison herd. Horseback riding is available along with a petting zoo. The park is located at 2272 North Coley Road and admission is required. Contact (662) 844-8709 or (866) 272-4766 for hours.

Bryce's Crossroads National Battlefield is located just north of Tupelo near Baldwyn and is the site where an outnumbered Confederate crew defeated Union forces in a Civil War battle in June of 1864. The Confederate victory at Brice's Cross Roads was a significant victory for Major General Nathan Bedford Forrest, but the victory did not help the Confederates in the long run. There are no visitor facilities at the battlefield site, however the site does contain three battlefield trails, interpretive markers, and two cemeteries located on 1,600 acres. The site is administered by the Natchez Trace Parkway and is located on Highway 370. **Bryce's Crossroads Visitor and Interpretive Center** is located several miles to the east near the intersection of Highway 45 and Highway 370 in Baldwyn. The center has interactive exhibits, dioramas, videos, and maps. Hours: Tue.-Sat. 9-5 P.M. The address is 607 Grisham Street. Contact (662) 365-3969. The **Natchez Trace Parkway Visitor Center** in Tupelo also has information about Bryce's Crossroads.

FESTIALS AND EVENTS

The annual **Tupelo Elvis Festival** is a celebration in honor of Elvis Presley and his music. The festival features live performances from local, regional, and national musicians along with local food vendors, a carnival midway, pet parade, beauty pageant, 5K run and more. The festival is held in early June. Contact (662) 841-6598.

The annual **Tupelo Film Festival** is a three-day event held in April and features independent films in a variety of genres from around the world. Established in 2004, the award-winning festival is held at the Tupelo Malco Cinema. Contact (800) 533-0611.

The annual **Gumtree Arts Festival** is held in Tupelo and features art vendors and over 100 art exhibitions from the region and beyond. The festival also offers food vendors, live music, and entertainment along with thousands of visitors. The festival has been a tradition since 1971 and is held in May at the Old Courthouse Square. Contact (662) 844-2787.

DINING IN TUPELO

For dining options in Tupelo, try **Kermit's Outlaw Kitchen** at 124 West Main Street for great American dishes. Hours: Mon.-Fri. 11-10:30 P.M., Sat. 11-11:30 P.M., Sun. 11-10:30 P.M. Contact (662) 620-6622. Also try the **Grill at Fairpark** at 343 East Main Street for a variety of American cuisine. Hours: Mon.-Sat. 11-10 P.M., Sun. 11-9 P.M. Contact (662) 680-3201.

CORINTH

HISTORY

Corinth was founded in 1853 as Cross City because of the location at the junction of the Mobile and Ohio railroad and the Memphis and Charleston railroad in the northeast corner of Mississippi. Corinth was later named after the Greek city Corinth that also served as a crossroads. The location of Corinth at the junction of two major railroads made the city strategically important to the Confederacy during the Civil War. Confederate General P.G.T. Beauregard retreated to Corinth after the Battle of Shiloh in Tennessee as he was pursued by Union Major General Henry W. Halleck. General Beauregard abandoned the town when General Halleck approached and the city came under Union control during the first **Battle of Corinth** (also known as the Siege of Corinth) in May of 1862. A second battle took place in October of 1862 when Confederate General Earl Van Dorn attempted to retake the city, however Union forces were successful in forcing out the Confederates. Today, Corinth has the largest number of intact Civil War earthworks in the nation, which were constructed by Confederate and Union armies.

ATTRACTIONS IN CORINTH

The **Corinth Visitors Bureau** is located at 215 North Fillmore Street. Contact (662) 287-8300 or (800) 748-9048.

The **Corinth Civil War Interpretive Center** is a division of the Shiloh National Military Park, which is located 22 miles to the northeast of Corinth in Tennessee. The Corinth center opened in 2004 near the site of Battery Robinett, which was a Union fortification where some of the most intense fighting took place during the Battle of Corinth. This 15,000 square foot facility features interactive exhibits which interpret the key role of Corinth in the Civil War. The rail crossing at Corinth ranked second only to the Confederate capital at Richmond in terms of strategic importance for more than a six month period of 1862. During the war, Corinth was fortified heavily by both Union and Confederate forces. The interpretive center grounds feature bronze reproduction artifacts on a walkway leading to the facility and six bronze life size statues of Civil War soldiers. Inside the center two professionally made videos of the battles of Shiloh and Corinth are shown. The center is located at 501 West Linden Street in Corinth and admission is free. Hours: 8-5 P.M. Contact (662) 287-9273.

Corinth National Cemetery was established in 1866 as a central burial site for 2,300 Union casualties in the Battle of Corinth and similar battles in the area. By 1870, there were more than 5,600 burials at the cemetery, most of which were unknown soldiers who came from 15 different states. The cemetery is located at 1551 Horton Street. Hours: daily 8-5 P.M. Contact (901) 386-8311.

The **Crossroads Museum** is housed in the historic Corinth railroad depot (1918) located at the crossroads of the two major railroads in town. The museum focuses on "all things Corinth" including the history of the city with exhibits on Civil War and railroad history, geology, and famous citizens of Corinth. The museum is located at 221 North Fillmore Street. Hours: Mon.-Sat. 10-4 P.M., Sun. 1-4 P.M. Contact (662) 287-3120.

The **Verandah House** was built in 1857 by Hamilton Mask and served as headquarters for Confederate and Union generals during the Civil War. Mask was a co-founder of the town of Corinth. The Greek Revival style home is a National Historic Landmark and is located at 705 Jackson Street. The home also contains 18th century and 19th century antiques and paintings. Tours are available by appointment. Contact (662) 287-8300.

DINING IN CORINTH

Established in 1865, **Borroum's** is Mississippi's oldest operating drug store and soda fountain. Dr. Andrew Jackson Borroum had just been released from a northern prison camp during the Civil War after having worked for both sides. On his way home, Borroum stopped in Corinth and decided to open an office for his pharmacy practice. Soon afterward Borroum opened a drug store because there was not one in town. The store also served as a general store in addition to a pharmacy throughout the years. Borroum's has continued to be operated by six generations of the Borroum family for 130 years. Today, the store looks very similar to the original store with historic memorabilia displayed inside. The store today is known for its **slugburger**, a sandwich made of ground beef or pork mixed with an extender such as soybeans or cornmeal and deep-fried in oil. Also known for their burgers and shakes, Borroum's is located at 604 Waldron Street. Hours: Mon.-Fri. 8-5 P.M., Sat. 8:30-3 P.M. Contact (662) 286-3361.

The annual **Slugburger Festival** is a three-day event held in Corinth in July. The event features live music and entertainment, a carnival, and food vendors selling a variety of foods. The festival has been a tradition since 1987. Contact (662) 287-8300.

Dilworth's Tamales is also a popular institution in town and is located at 111 Taylor Street. Open since 1962, Dilworth's continues to be operated by the same family in a drive-thru restaurant format. Tamales are traditionally made of cornmeal, ground meats, and spices wrapped in a corn husk (or parchment paper) and boiled or steamed. Hours: Mon.-Sat. 10-8 P.M., Sun. 2-6 P.M. Contact (662) 665-0833.

TISHOMINGO COUNTY

HISTORY

Tishomingo County is located at the northeast corner of Mississippi and is known for its natural beauty. Tishomingo County was formed in 1836 out of lands from the Chickasaw Cession of 1832. Resting on the foothills of the Appalachian Mountains, Tishomingo County offers two state parks, two major lakes, and the highest point in Mississippi at Woodall Mountain. Tishomingo County was also the location of the Battle of Iuka during the Civil War.

ATTRACTIONS

The **Tishomingo County Tourism Council** is located at 1001 Battleground Drive in Iuka and can provide information and maps. Contact (662) 423-0051 or (800) 386-4373.

Tishomingo State Park is located at the foothills of the Appalachian Mountains and is known not only for its history but its natural beauty. Evidence of ancient Native American civilization has been discovered here as early as 7,000 B.C. The park is named after the leader of the Chickasaw nation, Chief Tishomingo. The **Natchez Trace Parkway** runs directly through the park at milepost 304.5. Other roadways that lead to the park include Highway 25 from the north and south and Highway 30 from the west. The landscape of the park contains massive rock formations and steep rocky cliffs found nowhere else in Mississippi. Visitors to the park can see massive boulders covered in moss and hike trails once used by Native Americans.

Facilities and activities at Tishomingo State Park include campgrounds (including RV), cabins, fishing, boat launch, canoeing, and hiking trails. Six cabins are available near Bear Creek and are available for rent. The cabins contain bed and bath linens, kitchen equipment, air conditioning, heating, and stone fireplaces. Thirteen miles of hiking trails are available along rocky ridges with beautiful views, shallow canyons, natural springs, waterfalls, and the waters of Bear Creek.

A canoeing trip on **Bear Creek** is available for a fee from April to October. Scenic sandstone bluffs, hardwood and pine trees, shoals and rapids with long pools in between create an enjoyable experience. All supplies are provided by the park including canoes, paddles, lifejackets, and transportation. A swinging bridge made of native stone and steel cable crosses high above Bear Creek and is the entrance to hiking trails along the creek and along the top of the canyon walls. **Rock climbing** is permitted in the park but participants must provide their own equipment and secure a permit. **Haynes Lake** at the park contains catfish, bream, and bass for licensed fishers. Tishomingo State Park can be accessed from the Natchez Trace Parkway at milepost 304.5. Contact (662) 438-6914 for more information about Tishomingo State Park.

Bay Springs Lake is part of the Tennessee Tombigbee Waterway and is near Tishomingo County State Park to the west. Bay Springs Lake offers 6,700 acres of excellent recreation and fishing opportunities, a boat ramp, water skiing, canoeing, nature trails, and camping. The lake can be accessed from the Natchez Trace Parkway at milepost 293.4. The lake can also be accessed from Highway 30 or Highway 4. Contact (662) 423-0051 for more information.

Crow's Neck Environmental Education Center is located at Bay Springs Lake and offers interactive educational exhibits in a natural environment. Operated by Northeast Mississippi Community College, the center is located on 530 acres of rolling forested hills and the rugged shoreline of the lake. Crow's Neck is one of the Southeast's premier environmental education and conference centers for all ages and for professional and private gatherings. The center is located at 281 County Road 115. Hours: Mon.-Fri. 8-4:30 P.M. Contact (662) 438-6751 for more information.

Scenic **J.P. Coleman State Park** is located on a rocky bluff overlooking the Tennessee River and offers a variety of water sports on beautiful **Pickwick Lake**. The park and lake offer campgrounds (including RV), cabins, fishing, boating and boat launch, water skiing, and swimming. The park offers 20 cabins with beds and linens, kitchen equipment, air conditioning and heating. A motel at the park offers three luxury townhouses and 16 motel rooms that offer a view of the Tennessee River. Pickwick Lake offers 47,500 acres of freshwater for fishing and watersports. The lake offers crappie, bream, catfish, sauger, walleye, and most bass species for licensed fishers. The park is located on County Road 321 by way of Highway 25 north of Iuka. Contact (662) 423-6972 for more information.

Woodall Mountain is the highest elevation point in Mississippi at 807 feet and is located south of the city of Iuka. The mountain rises above the surrounding terrain so that it is visible for several miles. Woodall Mountain is classified as a monadnock, which is a ridge or small mountain that is composed of a rock that is more erosion resistant than the surrounding rock. Woodall Mountain is composed of sandstone with traces of iron which gives a rusty color to the rock and soil. It is believed that the Battle of Iuka took place near Woodall Mountain. Woodall Mountain can be located south of Iuka by way of Woodall Mountain Road. Contact (800) 386-4373 for more information.

BATTLE OF IUKA

The **Battle of Iuka** was a bloody clash occurring September 19, 1862 when Union General W. Rosecrans attempted to expel Confederate General Sterling Price from northeast Mississippi. About 6,000 men fought in the battle from both sides and in two hours 2,000 of the men perished. The battle was a victory for the Union and Rosecrans while the

Confederate forces fled. The **Tishomingo County Archives and History Museum** features artifacts from the Battle of Iuka and the Civil War in general. The museum is located inside the **Old Courthouse Museum,** a historic two story brick building built in 1888 and located at 203 East Quitman Street in Iuka. Admission is free. Hours: Tue.-Fri. 10-4 P.M. Contact (662) 423-3500.

The **Apron Museum** was opened in 2006 and claims to be the only museum in the world dedicated to aprons. The museum has thousands of aprons dating from the 1860's on display and for sale. The museum is located at 110 West Eastport Street in Iuka. Hours: Wed.-Fri. 9-5 P.M., Sat. 10-2 P.M. Contact (662) 279-2390.

DINING IN IUKA

For dining options in Tishomingo County, try the **Homestead Restaurant** at 1309 Battleground Drive in Iuka for Southern cuisine, steaks, seafood, soups, salads, sandwiches, and burgers. In addition to the menu, the restaurant offers a daily lunch buffet. Hours: Mon.-Tue. 11-8 P.M., Wed. 11-2 P.M., Thu.-Sat. 11-8 P.M., Sun. 11-2 P.M. Contact (662) 423-5577.

THE PINES REGION OF EAST MISSISSIPPI

The Pines region of Mississippi is located in the east central section of the state and the boundaries are south of Tupelo, east of Jackson, and north of Laurel. The region contains the cities of Meridian, Philadelphia, Choctaw, Kosciusko, Starkville, Columbus, Aberdeen, and Amory. The region also contains the Natchez Trace Parkway from Jackson to south of Tupelo. Highway 45 runs north-south and connects Corinth, Tupelo, Aberdeen, Columbus, and Meridian. Highway 82 runs east-west and connects Columbus and Starkville to Alabama and to Greenwood and the Delta region. Interstate 20 connects Meridian to Alabama and Jackson.

MERIDIAN

HISTORY

Meridian traces its history back to 1831, the year after the Choctaw Native Americans agreed to leave Mississippi according to the signing of the Treaty of Dancing Rabbit Creek. European Americans began to move to the area soon afterward. The city of Meridian was incorporated in 1860. Richard McLemore of Virginia was one of the first settlers to the area and he offered free land to attract more people to Meridian.

154

Railroads came to town in 1855 and since Meridian was located at a strategic location, the town grew significantly. During the Civil War, Meridian was the site of a Confederate arsenal, a military hospital, a prisoner-of-war stockade, and a number of state offices. In February 1864, General William Tecumseh Sherman and his Union army destroyed the city railroads and most of the surrounding area. The railroads were repaired quickly and the city continued to grow with the timber and cotton industry.

Meridian began its most progressive era from 1890 to 1930 when the city became Mississippi's largest city and one of the top manufacturing centers in the South. Much of the city skyline was built during this time including the Grand Opera House, the Threefoot building, and the Carnegie Library. Today, the economy has a strong manufacturing presence but has also developed a strong healthcare industry and is a large military employer with Meridian Naval Air Station and Key Field. The arts community in Meridian is strong with the Riley Center and the Meridian Museum of Art. Meridian is home to the only two row stationary Dentzel menagerie in existence. Peavey Electronics was founded by Hartley Peavey and is headquartered in Meridian.

Meridian has also produced many talented people. Known as the "Father of Country Music", Jimmie Rodgers was born in Meridian. Rodgers' music became popular in the 1920's and 1930's using vocal and guitar styles to produce a new type of music. Also from Meridian is Sela Ward, an Emmy Award winning actress.

ATTRACTIONS

The **Meridian Visitors Bureau** is located at 212 Constitution Avenue and can provide information, visitor guides, and maps. Contact (601) 482-8001 or (888) 868-7720.

Two Meridian residents set a world record in 1935. Brothers Fred and Al Key were co-managers of the struggling Meridian Airport and wanted to create attention to help the airport. The brothers broke the world endurance record for flight by circling the city of Meridian for over 653 hours inside a plane. The Key brothers broke the record by over 100 hours and were airborne for 27 days and nights non-stop. The flight totaled 52,320 miles, equal to twice the circumference of the Earth at the equator. A pictorial tribute exhibit is located at 2811 Highway 11 South at the Meridian Regional Airport. Contact (601) 482-0364.

The **Riley Center** is a major performing arts center, conference center, and education center located in historic downtown Meridian. One of the top performing arts centers in the Southeast, the center is housed in a beautiful state of the art historic building which was originally built in 1889 and was professionally restored in 2006 by Mississippi State University. The center offers world class cultural and artistic performances by nationally and internationally known performers as well as educational experiences, conferences, and meetings which attract over 60,000 visitors per year. The Riley Center includes a fully restored grand opera house theater that seats 950, a 200 seat studio theater, and 30,000 square feet of meeting space along with a large exhibit hall. The center is located at 2200 Fifth Street. Contact (601) 696-2220 for event times and ticket information.

Born in 1897 in Meridian, **Jimmie Rodgers** is known as the "Father of Country Music." Rodgers recordings of Southern blues and ballads greatly contributed to the popularity of a distinctively American musical form. Known for his "rhythmic yodeling," Rodgers began performing as early as the age of 13 while simultaneously working in the railroad industry, which was his father's profession. He became successful as a performer in the 1920's and 1930's, but suffered with tuberculosis for years and died in 1933 at age 35. Rodgers was one of the first three performers chosen for the Country Music Hall of Fame in 1961. He was also chosen to the Songwriters Hall of Fame in 1970 and to the Rock and Roll Hall of Fame in 1986. The museum contains artifacts, memorabilia, photos, and information about the life and career of Jimmie Rodgers including his original guitar, various railroading equipment, and memorials to the singer outside the museum. The museum is located inside Highland Park in Meridian at 1725 Jimmie Rodgers Memorial Drive and admission is charged. Hours: Tue.-Sat.10-4 P.M. Contact (601) 485-1808. (A cautionary note is that Highland Park is known to be located in a high crime section of town.)

Also inside Highland Park is **Dentzel Carousel**, the only remaining two row stationary Dentzel menagerie in the world. The carousel was built in 1896 for the 1904 St. Louis Exposition by Gustav Dentzel of Philadelphia, Pennsylvania. Dentzel owned a factory that produced carousels from 1860 to 1929. All of the animals on the carousel were hand carved out of wood and the carousels often had original oil paintings along with chariots. The carousel was purchased and shipped to Meridian and has been in operation since 1909. The carousel is housed inside a shelter building and was declared a National Historic Landmark in 1987. The carousel is housed in the only remaining carousel building constructed with a Dentzel blueprint. The carousel can be found at 1720 Jimmie Rodgers Memorial Drive. Hours: daily from June-July 1-5 P.M. April-May and August-October: Saturday and Sunday 1-5 P.M., November-March: Saturday only 1-5 P.M. Contact (601) 485-1802.

The **Temple Theater** was built in 1923 by the Hamasa Shriners in Moorish Revival style and is listed on the National Register of Historic Places. The theater was among the finest of its day, having one of the largest stage facilities in the United States. The theater contains a Robert Morton pipe organ and hosts live performances including stage shows, plays, and concerts. The theater is located at 2320 8th Street in Meridian. Contact (601) 693-1361 or (800) 243-1361 for show times.

The **Meridian Museum of Art** is housed inside the old Carnegie Library Building, which was constructed in 1912. The building is listed on the National Register of Historic Places and is a Mississippi Landmark. The museum hosts changing exhibitions focusing on artwork from Mississippi and Alabama artists while the permanent collection

157

focuses on Mississippi and regional artwork. The collections include a variety of art types including decorative arts, photography, crafts, and ethnographic and tribal materials. The museum is located at 628 25th Avenue and admission is free. Hours: Wed.-Sat. 11-5 P.M. Contact (601) 693-1501.

Merrehope Mansion was one of only six remaining antebellum buildings in Meridian after General Sherman's raid in 1864 during the Civil War. Built in 1858 by W.H. Jackson, this Greek Revival style mansion was used by Confederate Commander Leonidas Polk during the Civil War to house his family and as a headquarters. The mansion was also used as a shelter by several Union officers when they attacked the city in the Battle of Meridian. After the war, the mansion changed ownership several times and in 1968 the Meridian Restorations Foundation purchased the mansion and began the restoration process. The mansion is located at 905 Martin Luther King Jr. Drive and admission is required. Contact (601) 483-8439 for tour information.

FESTIVALS AND EVENTS

The annual **Threefoot Arts Festival** in downtown Meridian is held in early April and features regional arts and crafts, children's activities, food vendors, and live music and entertainment. The festival is named after the Threefoot building, which is the tallest building in Meridian. Contact (601) 693-2787.

The annual **Jimmie Rodgers Festival** is a three-day music festival held in May which honors Meridian native Jimmie Rodgers, who is known as the Father of Country Music and influenced musicians of all genres. A variety of regionally and nationally known musicians are invited to perform at the event. Contact (601) 485-1808.

The annual **State Games of Mississippi** began in 1992 as an Olympic-style event with 1,200 amateur athletes competing in 12 sports. Today, the State Games include 37 sports and more than 5,000 athletes competing. The State Games are a private non-profit organization that promotes amateur athletics and healthy lifestyles. The games are held in Meridian in June. Contact (601) 482-0205.

OUTDOOR RECREATION

Several outdoor recreational attractions are located near Meridian. **Dunn's Falls** is a 65 foot waterfall created in the 1850's by diverting a stream over a bluff and into the Chunky River. John Dunn, an Irish immigrant, created the waterfall to power a grist mill. The site contains a park where visitors can enjoy wildlife, picnic areas, the gristmill pond, hiking trails, cabins, primitive camping and swimming. The historic gristmill on site is not the original one but is an 1850's gristmill that was imported from Georgia. The park is located at 6890 Dunn Falls Road in Enterprise, Mississippi (just south of Meridian) and admission is charged. Contact (601) 655-8550 or (800) 748-9403 for more information.

The **Chunky River** is a popular canoeing destination in the summer months when the water is at low level. The Chunky River is a state designated scenic stream with rock outcrops. The river is located west of Meridian and can be accessed from Dunn's Falls or from Interstate 20 near the town of Chunky at exit 121. Canoe and kayak rental is available. Contact (601) 616-1616. The river can also be accessed from Interstate 59 at exit 142. Contact (601) 481-4210. A recreational site is located along the Chunky River's west bank at 24055 Highway 80 and features campsites and canoe and kayak rental. Contact (601) 480-3045.

Lake Okatibbee is a beautiful 3,800 acre lake that offers boating and boat launch, fishing, picnicking, bird viewing, swimming, and water skiing. RV campsites are available. The lake is located northwest of Meridian from Highway 19 at 9283 Pine Springs Road. Contact (601) 737-2370.

For dining options in Meridian try **Weidmann's** restaurant at 210 22nd Avenue for Southern comfort cuisine. Hours: Mon.-Thu. 11-9:30, Fri.-Sat. 11-11 P.M., Sun. 10-2 P.M. Contact (601) 581-5770.

PHILADELPHIA

HISTORY

Incorporated in 1833, **Neshoba County** contains the city of Philadelphia and the Choctaw community. Neshoba is a Choctaw word meaning "wolf". Philadelphia became the county seat of Neshoba County in 1837. The Pearl River flows east to west through Neshoba County and was an important waterway for early settlers. No major Civil War battles occurred in Neshoba County. After the war, the timber industry was important for growth and more recently the economy has diversified. The development of Pearl River Resort has had a major effect on the local economy. Philadelphia is also known as the birthplace of country musician Marty Stuart. **Visitor information** is located at 256 West Beacon Street in Philadelphia. Contact (601) 656-1000 or (877) 752-2643.

ATTRACTIONS AND EVENTS

The **Neshoba County Fair** was established in 1889 in Philadelphia, Mississippi and is one of the largest yearly events held in Mississippi. The event is the largest campground fair in the United States and houses Mississippi's only licensed horse track. Also known as "Mississippi's Giant Houseparty", the fair could be described as a large social event where families reunite and socialize. The fairgrounds were listed to the National Register of Historic Places in 1980. The fair offers a variety of amusement rides, a variety of food choices, live music, arts and crafts exhibits, antique car shows, harness horse races and rodeos. The fair hosts political speeches as state, local, and sometimes national level politicians give speeches at the fair while media outlets from around the state cover the speeches. In 1980, Ronald Reagan spoke at the fair before being elected president. The week-long event traditionally takes place in late July and early August. The fairgrounds are located southwest of Philadelphia at 16800 Highway 21 South and tours of the fairgrounds are available. Contact (601) 656-1000 or (877) 752-2643.

The **Mississippi Band of Choctaw Indians** is the only federally recognized Native American tribe living in Mississippi and has a membership of approximately 10,000. Choctaw lands cover over 35,000 acres in ten counties in Mississippi, with many living in Neshoba County. Most of the Choctaw Indian nation moved to Oklahoma in the 1830's through a series of treaties but some refused to leave. The descendants of these are the members of the Mississippi Band of Choctaw Indians. The Choctaw Indians operate the **Pearl River Resort**, which is located near Philadelphia and features several casinos, golf courses, a major waterpark, a spa, and retail shops. Contact (601) 656-5251 for more information about the Choctaw Indian Reservation.

Geyser Falls Water Theme Park is one of the top water theme parks in the Southeast. The 23 acre park features a variety of water themed attractions for children and adults including 13 large water slides, a wave pool, a river, eight acres of white sand beaches surrounding water pools, and a lake. The park also offers food and concessions. The park is located at 209 Black Jack Road from Highway 16 west of Philadelphia. Contact (601) 389-3100 or (866) 447-3275 for hours and ticket information.

Dancing Rabbit Golf Club is home to one of the top golf course venues in Mississippi and is ranked as one of the top 100 public courses in the nation. Located in a terrain of rolling hills are two par 72 courses, the Azaleas and the Oaks, which were designed by Tom Fazio and Jerry

Pate. The courses are located on Highway 16 west of Philadelphia. Contact Pearl River Resort at (866) 447-3275 for more information.

The **Choctaw Museum** was established in 1981 to promote knowledge and appreciation of the Choctaw culture. The museum focuses on the history and government of the Choctaw Indians, craft demonstrations, traditional art forms, and offers souvenir items for sale. The museum is located at 101 Industrial Road west of Philadelphia. Hours: 8-4:30 P.M. Contact (601) 650-1685.

Nanih Waiya is the site of an earthwork burial mound produced by ancient ancestors of the Choctaw Indians 1,700 to 2,000 years ago. The mound is important to the tribe's origin and the Choctaw believe the Nanih Waiya site is their Mother Mound. Nanih Waiya is the largest of the mounds at 25 feet tall, 140 feet wide, and 220 feet long. Several smaller mounds nearby have been nearly leveled by plowing. The site is located about 18 miles northeast of Philadelphia by way of Highway 21 and County Road 393. Contact (601) 656-5251 for more information.

The annual **Choctaw Indian Fair** is held in Neshoba County in July to celebrate the Choctaw heritage and culture. The four-day fair features tribal arts and crafts, traditional foods, dancing, cultural demonstrations, and the World Series of Stickball. The fair has been a tradition since 1949. Contact (601) 650-7450.

The **Williams Brothers General Store** has been in business since 1907 and was founded by the grandfather of current owner Sid Williams. The store was featured in a National Geographic magazine article in 1939 and the appearance of the store has not changed much since then. The store sells a variety of items from grocery foods to clothing and household items. A popular item is Wisconsin hoop cheese. Other food items at the store include deli meats and fresh produce. The store also sells shoes, boots, clothing, children's shoes, hardware and fencing materials, farm and garden supplies. The store is located at 10360 County Road 375 near Philadelphia. Hours: Mon.-Sat. 7-6 P.M. Contact (601) 656-2651.

KOSCIUSKO

HISTORY AND ATTRACTIONS

Kosciusko is located on the Natchez Trace Parkway between Jackson and Tupelo. Known as the birthplace of Oprah Winfrey and James Meredith, Kosciusko is the largest city on the Trace between Jackson and Tupelo and is a good stopping point along the way. Originally known as Redbud Springs, Kosciusko is named after Polish general Tadeusz Kosciuszko, who assisted the United States military during the Revolutionary War. Kosciusko is the county seat of Attala County and features a beautiful historic courthouse with a clock tower located in the downtown courthouse square. Attala County was named after a fictional Native American character in a 19th century novel.

The **Kosciusko Welcome Center** is located on the Natchez Trace Parkway at milepost 160. Hours: Daily 9-4 P.M. Contact (662) 289-2981. For dining options in Kosciusko, try the **Old Trace Grill** at 719 Veterans Memorial Drive for great southern cuisine. Hours: Tue.-Sat. 10:30-9 P.M. Contact (662) 289-2652.

The annual **Natchez Trace Festival** is held in Kosciusko in April and features live music, arts and craft vendors, children's activities, and more. The festival has been a tradition since 1969 and is held in historic downtown Kosciusko. Contact (662) 289-2981.

The **Central Mississippi Fair** is an annual week-long event held in August and features a variety of attractions including carnival rides, live music and entertainment, art shows, and livestock shows. The fair has been a tradition in Kosciusko for over 105 years. Contact (662) 289-2981.

FRENCH CAMP

HISTORY AND ATTRACTIONS

French Camp is a small historic town located at milepost 180.7 on the Natchez Trace Parkway. French Camp was originally a French settlement as Frenchman Louis Lefleur established a trading post and inn on the Natchez Trace in 1810. In 1885, a group of Scottish-Irish Christians established a girls school at French Camp. Soon a boys school was also established and in 1915 both schools were combined as **French Camp Academy**. About 300 people live and work at the academy and the town of French Camp has a population of about 150, many of whom attend or work at the academy.

The **French Camp Historic District** includes several log cabins including the **Alumni Museum** (1885), which was built by Francis Asbury Allen and was eventually donated to French Camp Academy. The district also includes the **Blacksmith Shop** and the restored **Post Office**, which served the town for over 70 years and is now a pottery studio. The **Drane House** is an antebellum home (1845) in the district and was owned by former Mississippi State Representative Colonel James Drane. The **Carriage House** is a bed and breakfast cabin which houses a carriage once owned by Greenwood Leflore. Leflore was the Choctaw Indian Chief who negotiated the Treaty of Dancing Rabbit Creek with President Andrew Jackson.

The **Council House Café** inside the historic district offers sandwiches, salads, soups, and deserts. The café is housed inside a cabin that once was a meeting place for Greenwood Leflore and his chiefs during tribal negotiations. The café is open Monday through Saturday 10:30-7 P.M.

The French Camp Historic District is located at 55 LeFleur Circle. Contact (662) 547-6835 for more information.

Rainwater Observatory and Planetarium is an educational ministry of French Camp Academy and features the largest observatory in Mississippi. The observatory assists several groups and organizations including universities, museums, science centers, schools, churches, scouting and civic groups, and hosts up to 200 groups per year. The 16 foot telescope at the observatory was purchased in 1985 from a Jesuit priest in Booneville, Mississippi and placed on an open ridge on the academy's property. Today, the observatory has 24 telescopes and optical instruments which make up the largest and most powerful collection in Mississippi. The largest telescope is a 32 inch Tectron with an automation system. The planetarium has a six meter dome and a Spitz A-2 projector. The planetarium can seat up to 50 people and also features museum exhibits including an extensive meteorite collection. The observatory is located on Highway 413 just off the Natchez Trace Parkway. Contact (662) 547-6377 for tours.

STARKVILLE

HISTORY

Starkville is the county seat of Oktibbeha County and is located on land that was once inhabited by Choctaw Indians. The first European Americans to settle in Oktibbeha County were Presbyterian missionaries led by Cyrus Kingsbury in 1820. The Choctaws left in 1830 after the Treaty of Dancing Rabbit Creek. Afterward many settlers came and the settlement was called Boardtown. Oktibbeha County was founded in 1833 and in 1835 the county seat was established at Boardtown, which was renamed Starkville in honor of Revolutionary War Hero John Stark. Oktibbeha was a Choctaw name meaning "icy waters". Starkville grew as an agricultural community with cotton and livestock. The Civil War was a setback for the county and city as many volunteered for the war and Union Colonel Benjamin H. Grierson and his forces raided town.

After the war, the first railroads were built in Starkville in the 1870's including the Gulf, Mobile, and Ohio railroad from Artesia. In 1875, a fire on Main Street destroyed 52 buildings but eventually the buildings were rebuilt. In 1878, Mississippi Agricultural and Mechanical College was established and would later become the economic driver of Starkville as Mississippi State University. Starkville would grow substantially after 1900 as people moved from rural areas into town and with growth from the university.

ATTRACTIONS

Tourist information and maps can be found at 200 East Main Street in Starkville. Contact (662) 323-3322 or (800) 649-8687.

The historic **John M. Stone Cotton Mill** was built in 1902 and was named after former Mississippi Governor John Marshall Stone. The

166

iconic brick cotton mill has a tower in the front center of the building and has in general two floors with a portion of a third floor on the east side. The building operated as a cotton mill until 1962. Mississippi State University purchased the building, which sits across the street from campus, in 1965 to house various campus departments and was named the E.E. Cooley Building. In 2014, a major renovation project began to convert the former mill into a major conference center with office space and an adjacent hotel. The building is located at the intersection of Highway 12 and Russell Street. Contact (662) 325-2323 for more information.

The **Cullis Wade Depot Welcome Center** on the Mississippi State University Campus has information and maps for university events, museums, and attractions. Also inside the welcome center is the **Cullis and Gladys Wade Clock Museum**, which features a large selection of over 400 antique wall clocks and watches dating from the 1700's. Above the welcome center on the second floor is an art gallery which offers changing exhibitions. The building also features a two story Barnes and Noble bookstore, which is located at 75 B.S. Hood Road. Welcome Center hours are Mon.-Fri. 8-5 P.M. Contact (662) 325-2323 for more information.

Known as the **MSU Cheese Shop**, the Mississippi Agricultural and Forestry Experiment Station or MAFES sales store offers a variety of cheese, ice cream, juice, jelly, and meat for sale. The cheese is often given as a gift to family and friends and can be ordered online or purchased inside the store, which is located at the Herzer Dairy Science building at 925 Stone Boulevard. Hours: Mon.-Fri. 8-5 P.M. Contact (662) 325-2338.

The **Mitchell Memorial Library** offers several major museums and attractions in addition to serving as the main library for Mississippi State University. The library is located at 395 Hardy Road. Contact (662) 325-7668.

The **Ulysses S. Grant Presidential Library** is located on the first floor of Mitchell Memorial Library and is home to 17,000 linear feet of memorabilia once belonging to the former president and Civil War general, including papers and photographs. The papers document important periods in United States history in the 19th century including the Mexican War, the Civil War, the Gilded Age, and European issues. Mississippi State University is one of only five universities nationwide to host a presidential library. Hours: Mon.-Fri. 7:30-5 P.M. Contact (662) 325-4552 for more information.

The **John Grisham Room** is focused on best-selling author, former Mississippi legislator, and Mississippi State alumnus John Grisham. The room contains materials and memorabilia from the writings and achievements of Grisham including photographs, subject files, original manuscripts of Grisham's first novel, *A Time to Kill*, fan mail and personal letters, newspaper clippings, and promotional materials. The Grisham Room is located inside Mitchell Memorial Library on the third floor. Hours: Mon.-Fri. 8-5 P.M. Contact (662) 325-6634.

The **Charles H. Templeton, Sr. Music Museum** features a collection of musical instruments, recordings, and sheet music by Starkville businessman Charles H. Templeton, Sr. The collection includes over 200 instruments from 1897 to the 1930's including Thomas Edison's early model phonographs, Eldridge Johnson's gramophones, Columbia graphophones, a vintage Link player piano, an Aeolion Orchestrelle player organ, cylinder-and-disc music boxes, and organettes of paper roll and cob varieties. The museum is located inside Mitchell Memorial Library on the fourth floor. Hours: Mon.-Fri. 9-4 P.M. Contact (662) 325-6634.

Historic Lee Hall is a five story landmark building on campus that houses the **Bettersworth Auditorium** and several academic departments. The auditorium is a 1,000 seat theater that hosts several performing arts events throughout the year in addition to speeches by nationally known figures. The university hosts the annual **Lyceum**

Series, which is a series of performing arts events by nationally or regionally known performers and is held throughout the year on campus. Contact (662) 325-2930 for Lyceum Series events and times. Lee Hall is located at 262 Lee Boulevard and is part of the historic campus surrounding the main quadrangle greenspace known as the **Drill Field**. Contact (662) 325-2323 for information about Lee Hall or the Drill Field.

STARKVILLE DISTRICTS

The **Old Main District** in Starkville houses the oldest business district in the city and includes professional and law offices, banks, local shops, restaurants, and local government facilities. **Reed's Department Store** offers upscale clothing and sportswear for men, women, and children at 302 University Drive. Hours: Mon.-Sat. 9:30-6 P.M. Contact (662) 323-2684. **Sullivan's Office Supply** is a downtown fixture specializing in professional office supplies and furniture. Sullivan's is located at 204 Main Street. Hours: Mon.-Fri. 8:30-5:30 (Sat. 10-4 P.M.). Contact (662) 323-5222.

The historic **Hotel Chester** is located at the corner of Main Street and Jackson Street and was built in 1925 as a full service hotel. The **Beer Garden Restaurant** inside Hotel Chester was designed by world renowned chef Gordon Ramsay and features an outdoor patio. Contact (662) 323-5005 or (866) 325-5005. Restaurant Hours: Mon.-Thu. 4 P.M.-12 A.M., Fri.-Sat. 4 P.M.-1 A.M. Other popular restaurants and nightspots on Main Street include **Mugshots Grill**, **Restaurant Tyler**, and **Old Venice**.

The **Cotton District** is located between the Old Main District and the Mississippi State University campus and features a mix of residential and commercial properties along University Drive. The district is heavily populated with university students and features several restaurants and businesses which cater to the student population. Popular restaurants include **City Bagel Café, Bin 612, Stromboli's,** and **Bulldog Deli,** all of which are located on University Drive. **Little Dooey's** Barbeque is a popular place located just off University Drive on Fellowship Street. Unique architectural styles can be found in the Cotton District, which has been the product of developer and former mayor Dan Camp. The district has been featured in national magazines and the architectural styles have been studied by universities and other groups across the country.

The Starkville area does have several antebellum homes but most are not available to the public. One exception is the **Cedars**, built in 1836 with Late Colonial and Greek Revival architecture. The home features seven hand carved fireplace mantles and four bedrooms which are available as a bed and breakfast combination. The home is located at 6149 Oktoc Road. Contact (662) 324-7569. Another bed and breakfast in Starkville is **Magnolia Manor**, a restored early 1900's mansion located at 215 North Jackson Street. Contact (662) 694-1832.

FESTIVALS AND EVENTS

The annual **Magnolia Independent Film Festival** is held in February in Starkville and features a variety of independent films. The festival is held at Hollywood Premier Cinema on Stark Road. Contact (662) 324-3080.

The annual **Cotton District Arts Festival** is held in Starkville in April and features arts and crafts vendors, live music, a 5K run, and food vendors from area restaurants. Contact (662) 324-3080.

DINING IN STARKVILLE

For dining options in Starkville, restaurants on Main Street and University Drive tend to cater to the university crowd. Restaurants outside these districts include the **Veranda Restaurant**, which is a popular restaurant located at 208 Lincoln Green. The Veranda specializes in steaks and southern comfort food in a casual dining atmosphere. Hours: Mon.-Thu. 11-12 A.M., Fri.-Sat. 11-1 A.M., Sun. 10-10 P.M. Contact (662) 323-1231.

Harvey's Restaurant is another popular casual dining establishment located at 406 Highway 12 and specializes in steaks, pasta, and seafood. Harvey's is located at 406 Highway 12. Hours: Mon.-Thu. 11-9:30 P.M., Fri.-Sat. 11-10 P.M., Sun. 11-9 P.M. Contact (662) 323-1669.

COLUMBUS

HISTORY

Columbus is located at the junction of three rivers, the Tombigbee, the Buttahatchie, and the Luxapalila. The area now known as Columbus was mentioned in the writings of Hernando de Soto, who is believed to have crossed the Tombigbee River in 1540. A trading post was located here as early as the 1780's and the city of Columbus was chartered in 1821. The first public school in Mississippi was founded in Columbus at Franklin Academy, and is still in operation. The Treaty of Dancing Rabbit Creek opened up more land for settlers in 1830. The rich black prairie soil around Columbus attracted wealthy cotton planters from the East Coast. By the 1850's, Columbus was a boomtown as a result of cotton production.

During the Civil War, Columbus maintained an arsenal that made gunpowder, handguns, and cannons. Because of this, Union army forces repeatedly tried to invade Columbus, but were stopped by Confederate forces under the command of General Nathan Bedford Forrest. Because of this and the city's status as a hospital town, most of the antebellum homes were preserved and today Columbus has the second largest collection in Mississippi behind Natchez.

Columbus is credited with inspiring the tradition of Memorial Day. After the Civil War, women in Columbus decorated the graves of both Confederate and Union soldiers at Friendship Cemetery. This act of kindness was celebrated in the poem, The *Blue and the Gray* by Francis Miles Finch of New York, who read of the act in the New York Tribune. **Friendship Cemetery** was founded in 1849 and is located at Fourth Street and 15th Avenue. Contact (662) 328-4164 for more information.

The first state-supported college for women was organized in 1884 in Columbus and is known today as **Mississippi University for Women**. The university is located at 1100 College Street. Contact (662) 329-4750. **Franklin Academy** was the first free public school in Mississippi, opening in 1821 and is open today at 501 Third Avenue. Contact (662) 241-7151. Today, Columbus has a large collection of antebellum homes, several of which are available for tours. Visitor information and maps can be obtained at the **Visitors Bureau** at 117 Third Street or at the Tennessee Williams Welcome Center at 300 Main Street. Contact (662) 329-1191 or (800) 327-2686. Columbus hosts a **spring pilgrimage** every year to showcase the antebellum homes in the city.

HISTORIC ATTRACTIONS

The **Tennessee Williams Welcome Center** is the first home of Pulitzer Prize winning playwright, Tennessee Williams. Williams was born in Columbus in 1911 and produced famous works such as *A Streetcar Named Desire* and *The Glass Menagerie*. The home (1875) was moved from its original location in 1993 to a new location at 300 Main Street and received a renovation. The home was designated a National Literary

Landmark and now serves as a welcome center for the city of Columbus. Hours: Mon.-Sat. 8:30-5 P.M. Contact (662) 328-0222.

The **Lowndes County Courthouse** was built in 1847 and was designed by local architect James Lull. The Mississippi Legislature met here after Jackson fell into Union control during the Civil War. The courthouse is located at 505 Second Avenue. Contact (662) 329-1191 for more information.

The **Cartney-Hunt House** is a Federal style house built in 1828 and is the oldest brick house in north Mississippi. Built by James M. Cartney, the house was restored by a local attorney in 1983 and currently operates as a bed and breakfast. The house has won restoration awards and is listed on the National Register of Historic Places. The house is located at 408 Seventh Street. Contact (662) 244-7232 or (800) 327-2686 for more information.

Rosedale (built in 1856) is an excellent example of Italianate architecture and is considered one of the finest in Mississippi. The home also has a large collection of American-made antiques and is located at 1523 Ninth Street. Contact (662) 328-0222 or (800) 327-2686 for tour information.

Rosewood Manor and Gardens is a beautiful Greek Revival style mansion built in 1835 and has been featured in several publications. The mansion contains period furnishings and landscaped gardens. The mansion is located at 719 Seventh Street. Contact (662) 328-7313 or (662) 364-0705 for tour information.

The **Amzi Love Home** was built in 1848 and eight generations of family continue to live in the home. The family residents are descendants of Amzi Love and his wife Edith Wallace. The home is located at 305 Seventh Street and contains original furnishings. The **Lincoln Home** is connected to the Amzi Love Home by beautiful gardens. The Lincoln Home operates as a bed and breakfast and once was home to an early mayor of Columbus. The home is located at 714 Third Avenue. Contact (662) 328-5413 or (800) 327-2686.

The **Stephen D. Lee Home** was built by Major Thomas Blewett in 1847 and was the residence of Confederate General Stephen D. Lee. The home is now a museum housing Civil War collections and artifacts. The home is located at 316 Seventh Street. Contact (662) 435-2368 for tour information.

Temple Heights was built in 1837 and combines Federal and Greek Revival styles along with four floors, porches, and 14 Doric columns. The home includes period furnishings and a decorative arts collection is located inside. The home has been featured in national magazines and Home and Garden Television. Temple Heights is located at 515 Ninth Street. Contact (662) 328-0599 or (800) 327-2686 for tour information.

Whitehall is a two story mansion built in 1843 with the Greek Revival style by James Walton Harris. The mansion features six paneled, square columns at the edge of a wooden porch. The mansion is located at 607 Third Street. Contact (662) 328-0222 or (800) 327-2686 for tours.

Shadowlawn Mansion was built in 1848 by Benjamin Catley and today operates as a bed and breakfast. The recently restored mansion showcases Italianate, Greek Revival, and Gothic Revival styles. The mansion has been featured on national television network HGTV and is located at 1024 College Street. Contact (662) 327-3600 for tours or lodging information.

FESTIVALS AND EVENTS

The annual **Spring Pilgrimage** in Columbus features a tour of historic antebellum homes and gardens with carriage rides and bus rides. The Pilgrimage is held in April. Contact (662) 329-1191.

The annual **Market Street Festival** is held in downtown Columbus in early May and features arts and crafts, food vendors, and live music. The festival has been a tradition since 1995. Contact (662) 328-6305.

Columbus also hosts a **Tennessee Williams Tribute** to honor poet and playwright Tennessee Williams in September. The tribute features dramatic presentations, scholarly lectures, and presentations associated with the works of Williams, who was born in Columbus. The event also includes a tour of Victorian homes in Columbus. Contact (800) 327-2686.

DINING IN COLUMBUS

For dining options in Columbus, try **Harvey's Restaurant** for great steaks, pasta, seafood, and American cuisine. Harvey's is located at 200 Main Street. Hours: Sun.-Thu. 11-9:30 P.M., Fri.-Sat. 11-10 P.M. Contact (662) 327-1639.

WEST POINT

HISTORY AND ATTRACTIONS

West Point is located at the intersection of Highway 45 and Highway 50 in East Mississippi. In addition to Waverly Mansion and the Prairie Arts Festival, West Point has an attractive downtown centered around Commerce Street. **Ritz Theatre** is a historic theater built in the 1930's at 125 Commerce Street. The theater was renovated into a conference center and an upscale restaurant, **Café Ritz**. Contact (662) 494-7489. For **tourist information** about West Point, contact (662) 494-5121.

West Point was also the hometown of Blues musician **Howlin' Wolf** and a yearly festival is held in his honor in late August near Labor Day.

The **Waverly Mansion** is one of the most photographed mansions in the South. Located 23 miles northwest of Columbus in West Point, Mississippi, the mansion was built in 1852 by Col. George Young. The mansion has been featured in many national and international magazines, in addition to the television network A&E show *American Castles*. The distinguishing feature of the mansion is the large octagonal shaped rotunda which projects from the center of the roof as a cupola. This structure combines ornament and technology in the tradition of Thomas Jefferson. The varied decorative treatment of each room was artistic and the lighting system (by using gas manufactured on the site) was scientific. The mansion has been fully restored by the Robert Snow family and has been declared a National Historic Landmark. The plantation also features a nationally known golf course which is also named Old Waverly. The mansion is located at 1852 Waverly Mansion Road off Highway 50. Contact (662) 494-1399 or (800) 327-2686. The mansion is open daily 9-5 P.M. for tours and admission is required.

FESTIVALS

The annual **Prairie Arts Festival** is held in downtown West Point in late August and features arts and crafts, food vendors, live music, and entertainment. The festival attracts over 400 exhibitors and has been named a Top Ten event by the Southeast Tourism Association. The festival has been a tradition since 1978. Contact (662) 494-5121.

ABERDEEN

HISTORY

Hernando De Soto passed by Aberdeen on the Tombigbee River in 1540 and was the first European explorer in the area. Aberdeen was first settled in 1834 and was founded in 1837. Aberdeen became the county seat of Monroe County when it was formed in 1849. Located on the banks of the Tombigbee River, Aberdeen was one of the busiest Mississippi ports in the 19th century. Cotton was the largest industry and Aberdeen was the second largest city in Mississippi at one time. Wealthy merchants and planters built large antebellum homes in town and today Aberdeen has many historic buildings, including 200 on the National Register of Historic Places.

ATTRACTIONS

Each year, Aberdeen hosts a **Spring Pilgrimage** tour of antebellum homes in April. Aberdeen has beautiful tree lined streets and a busy shopping district along **Commerce Street** in addition to the scenic Tennessee-Tombigbee Waterway. The historic **Elkin Theater** hosts movies, performing arts events, and community meetings at 110 W. Commerce Street. Opened in 1937, the theater is owned by the local group Aberdeen Elkin Theater Association. Contact (662) 369-9440 or (800) 634-3538.

The **Aberdeen Visitors Bureau** is located at 204 East Commerce Street and provides tourist information, home tours, and maps. Contact (662) 369-9440 or (800) 634-3538.

The **Magnolias** is one of the most prominent antebellum homes in Aberdeen. Built by Dr. and Mrs. William Alfred Sykes in the Greek Revival style in 1850, the home has a front portico along with Greek columns and a beautiful mahogany stairway. Five generations of the Sykes family lived in the home until 1984 when the home was sold to Clarence Day. After a large renovation project, the home was donated to the city of Aberdeen in 1986 in memory of Day's parents. The Magnolias is located at 732 West Commerce Street and tours are available by appointment. Contact (662) 369-7956 or (662) 369-9440.

Sunset Hill was originally built in 1847 by John Harris and was renovated in 1853 by William Redd Cunningham, who created the Greek Revival style of the home. Doric columns are featured on three sides of the landmark home, which is located at 803 West Commerce Street. Contact (662) 369-9440 for tour information.

Holiday Haven was built in 1850 and was part of the Holiday family until 1993. The home contains many original furnishings and this Greek Revival style home also features landscaped grounds. Holiday Haven is located at 609 South Meridian Street. Contact (662) 369-9440 for tour information.

Aberdeen Lake is a popular recreational attraction for fishing, boating, water skiing, and camping. The lake was created with a lock and dam on the Tennessee-Tombigbee River near Aberdeen. **Blue Bluff Recreation Area** on Aberdeen Lake offers RV hookups, hiking trails, boat ramps and docks. The bluff rises 80 feet above the lake and offers a scenic view. The recreational area can be accessed from Rye Road. Contact (662) 369-2832 or (800) 634-3538.

DINING IN ABERDEEN

For dining options in Aberdeen, try the **Friendship House Restaurant** for great steaks and seafood. The Friendship House is located at 20025 Doss Drive. Hours: Tue.-Sat. 5-9 P.M. Contact (662) 257-2211.

AMORY

HISTORY

Amory was the first planned city in Mississippi. The Kansas City, Memphis & Birmingham Railroad needed a midpoint between Memphis, Tennessee and Birmingham, Alabama for their locomotives. The new town of Amory was plotted in 1887 and was incorporated in 1888. People from nearby Cotton Gin Port on the Tombigbee River abandoned their town and moved to Amory. Amory visitor information can be found at 129 Main Street. Contact (662) 256-8700.

FESTIVALS AND ATTRACTIONS

The city of Amory holds an annual festival each April known as the **Amory Railroad Festival** in Frisco Park in downtown Amory to honor the culture and heritage of the city. The Railroad Festival includes southern foods such as fried catfish, barbecue, and apple fritters. In addition, the festival offers amusement rides, arts and crafts, and live music. Although the date of the festival in April often results in rain during one or more days of the three day festival, turnout is generally large, with thousands attending. The festival has been named a top 29 event by the Southeast Tourism Society and has been a tradition since 1979. Frisco Park is located at Main Street and 1st Avenue. Contact (662) 256-8700 for more information.

The **Amory Regional Museum** focuses on the history of the region and features a variety of exhibits. The museum building was originally built in 1916 as the Gilmore Sanitarium (a medical facility for chronic

179

illness). After becoming vacant in the 1970's, the building was donated to the Amory Arts Council and was converted into a museum. Today, the museum is a Mississippi Landmark and features contemporary artwork, photographs, and memorabilia from the history of Amory. The museum is located at 801 South Third Street. Hours: Tue.-Fri. 9-5 P.M., Sat. 10-4 P.M., Sun. 1-5 P.M. Contact (662) 256-2761.

DINING IN AMORY

For dining options in Amory, try **Bill's Hamburgers** at 310 Main Street. Bill's Hamburgers has been open since 1929 and was founded by Bob Hill. Bill's Hamburgers are cooked with fresh ground beef and the secret recipe, which has been passed down for generations. Hours: Mon.-Fri. 7:30-5:30 P.M., Sat. 7-5 P.M. Contact (662) 256-2085.

VARDAMAN

The annual Vardaman Sweet Potato Festival is a tradition that features a celebration of the sweet potato crop harvest. The town of Vardaman is known as the Sweet Potato Capital of the World and hosts a week-long celebration featuring arts and crafts, food vendors, live entertainment, beauty contests, eating contests, and a 5K run. A sweet potato tasting booth, a sweet potato pie eating contest, and barbeque chicken are available at the festival. Vardaman is located 10 miles west of Houston, Mississippi on Highway 8. The festival is held in November and has been a tradition since 1973. Contact (662) 682-7559.

MAPS

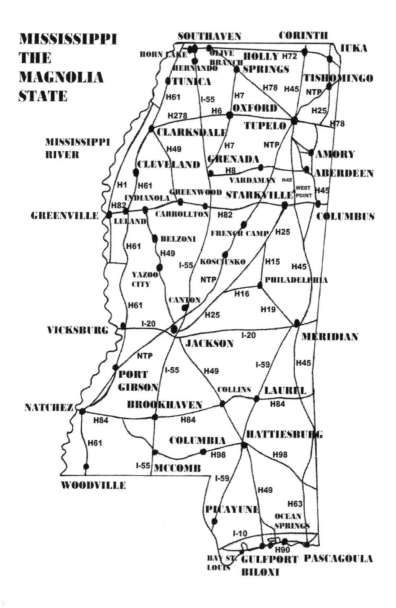

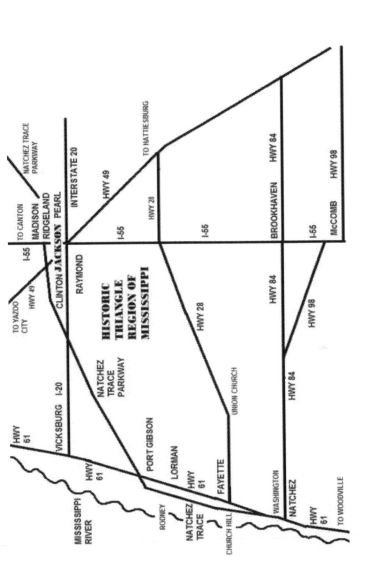

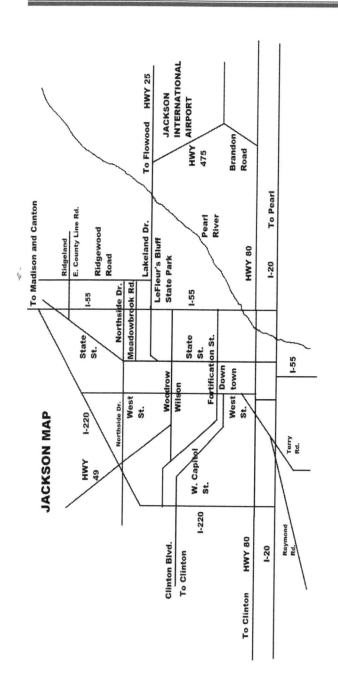

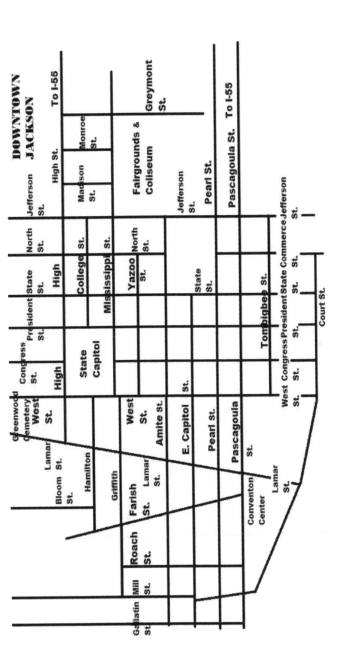

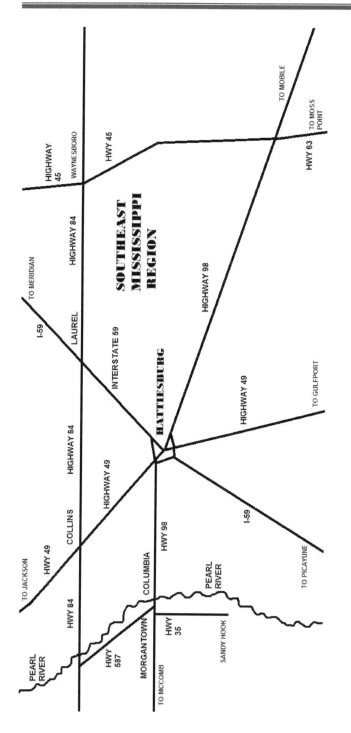

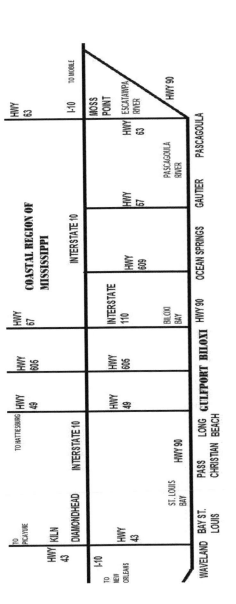

COASTAL REGION OF MISSISSIPPI

GULF OF MEXICO

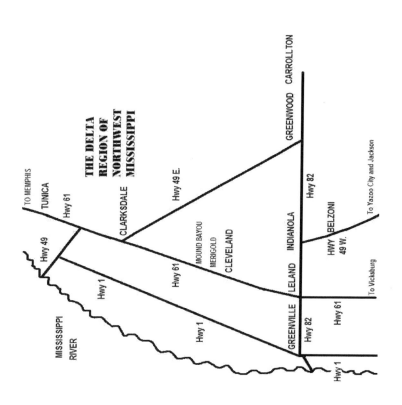

THE DELTA
REGION OF
NORTHWEST
MISSISSIPPI

TO MEMPHIS
TUNICA
Hwy 61
Hwy 49
CLARKSDALE
Hwy 49 E.
MISSISSIPPI
RIVER
Hwy 1
Hwy 61
MOUND BAYOU
MERIGOLD
CLEVELAND
Hwy 1
GREENWOOD
CARROLLTON
Hwy 82
INDIANOLA
To Yazoo City and Jackson
LELAND
HWY BELZONI
49 W.
To Vicksburg
GREENVILLE
Hwy 82
Hwy 61
Hwy 1

188

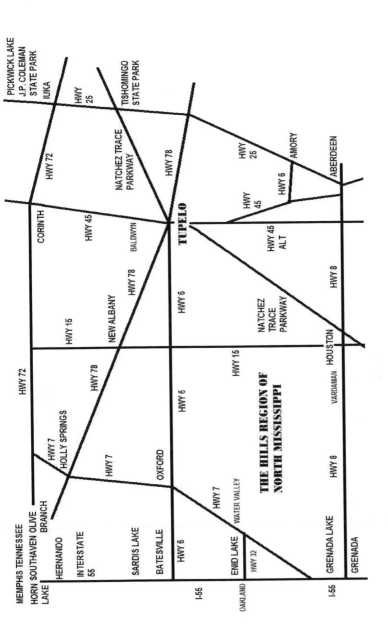

THE HILLS REGION OF
NORTH MISSISSIPPI

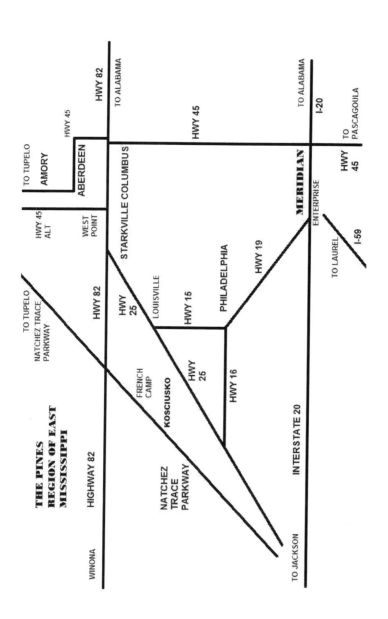

Made in the USA
San Bernardino, CA
04 March 2016